TURNING ON THE LIGHT

A Plan for Self Empowerment and Fullness of Life

Bob Earll

TURNING ON THE LIGHT

A Plan for Self Empowerment and Fullness of Life

TURNING ON THE LIGHT

A Plan for Self Empowerment and Fullness of Life

DEDICATION

EARLIER THIS YEAR WHEN OUR DAUGHTER ALEXANDRA — who prefers to be called Sasha — was twenty months old, she and her mother and I went for one of our pre-bedtime walks. We lived in the high desert and headed toward the mesas behind our house. There was a full moon in the making hanging over the mesa and we were aimed right for it. Sasha was walking between us, busy proclaiming "Walk self," which means "I don't want to hold hands and I don't want to be guided by your hands on my shoulders or your fingers at the back of my head." Occasionally her mother and I forget that she has her own speed and her own method and they work just fine for her.

A short way up the road she placed her arms in front of her- bent at the elbows-and began to roll them over each other like an old-fashioned lawn mower. Her eyes were alive with excitement and she repeated the phrase "Sasha flying" two or three times. Then she placed her arms straight out like wings and said "Sasha flying through the air" a couple of times.

Her expression was that of a child having the time of her life on a ride in an amusement park. After ten or fifteen seconds she extended her arms in front of her much as she does when she is indicating that she wants to be picked up and she announced, "Sasha holding the moom." Her mother and I looked down at this child holding the "moom" and started to cry. As far as we knew, this little free spirit might very well be holding the "moom."

I'd like to dedicate this book to the "walk self" fly to the "moom" spirit in everyone of us.

REVIEWS

Leaders in recovery have said this about Bob's first book, I Got Tired of Pretending:

"Besides being a wonderful speaker, Bob Earll is a wonderful writer. This book touches me where I most need to be touched, in the gut. This is a book that can heal!"

~John Bradshaw
Author of *Homecoming* and *Bradshaw On: The Family*

"Each time we hear a recovering person's story, we untangle more of the co-dependency trap. Bob Earll's openly shared story will help readers understand their own."

~Sharon Wegscheider-Cruse
Author of *Choicemaking*

"I Got Tired of Pretending is a solid example of good counsel and storytelling. The readers can easily find themselves in these stories and take both support and encouragement in their search for their understanding and recovery."

~Robert Subby
Author of *Lost in the Shuffle*

"I don't have many books on my 'must read' list, but I Got Tired of Pretending by Bob Earll is one. This is a book of the heart. What sets this book apart from other books about dysfunctional families is Bob's willingness to share his pain. This is a book of hope and triumph for adult children by an adult child!"

Bob Earll, a successful television writer for twenty years, has emerged as one of the most popular speakers and workshop leaders in the areas of dysfunctional families and codependency. Exploring his recovery for more than 29 years, Bob offers others a gift of truth and freedom.

In **Turning On The Light**, Bob Earll's second book, he offers a workable plan for incorporating some of the best elements of recovery, metaphysics and new age into the healing process. Having learned from the troubling consequences of distancing himself from his emotional and spiritual needs while in his own recovery program, Bob has constructed a tool kit for emotional and spiritual survival in the 90's.

"Bob Earll writes from his heart in ways that bless us all."

~HUGH PRATHER

Author of *Notes To Myself* and *A Book for Couples* (with Gayle Prather)

"Bob Earll's works are always a mixture of joy and pain. In *Turning on the Light* he challenges both the new-agers and diehard old 12 steppers to meet in the clearing and take the best from both worlds. His willingness to write on controversial subjects is refreshing."

~PIA MELLODY, R. N.,

Author of *Facing Codependence, Breaking Free* and *Facing Love Addiction*

"Bob Earll writes direct from the heart, humbly expressing his own experiences and feelings which will inspire and encourage the reader to discover and share their own inner feelings."

~BARRY AND JOYCE VISSELL

Authors of *The Shared Heart, Models of Love* and *Risk to be Healed*

ACKNOWLEDGMENTS

Tina, who lets me be me, and Sasha my teacher.

Tom Alibrandi, Bill O'Donnell Jr., Bob Crewe, Fred Altenhouse, David Hoobler, Larry Littlebird, Harold Littlebird, Larry Pierce and all of the rest of you who have shined your light on my path.

John Bradshaw, John Lee, Shakti Gawain, Bob Subby, Rokelle Lerner, Sharon Wegscheider-Cruse, Melody Beattie, Patrick Carnes, Pia Mellody, Judy Hollis, Emmett E. Miller, Ann Wilson Schaef, Sam Keen, Robert Bly, Michael Meade, Robert Moore, Stuart Wilde, Barry and Joyce Vissell, Hugh Prather, Scott Peck and all of the others who work so hard in these troubled times to bring light to others.

Thanks to the staff at Sierra Tucson to whom the words recovery and light are synonymous.

Susan Newcomer, my editor, with whom I dueled over commas and clarity. Thank you for your patience.

Last but not least, thanks to Phyllis, who has been there in the trenches.

INTRODUCTION

THE INFORMATION IN THIS BOOK has dramatically changed my life from one of pretense, fear, emptiness, shame, darkness and unhappiness to one of fulfillment on many levels.

The information in this book has changed the lives of thousands of others to one degree or another. In essence, the information comes from two large communities, both of equal importance, who are starting to make the world a better place to live. They are in possession of information and attitudes that can feed the hungry, house the homeless, heal the sick, win the drug war, stop child and spouse abuse and achieve world peace.

But they often find themselves frustrated not only in their progress but in their personal lives as well. They haven't been able to follow their hearts or their bliss (as Joseph Campbell so eloquently put it). Their achievements fall short of their expectations, their progress stalls, they start sliding backwards. The light is missing from their lives or keeps dimming and going out.

Despite a hundred thousand affirmations they still feel inadequate, flawed. Their relationships remain less than satisfactory or they don't have any. In an attempt to survive they have made a door-less prison out of rigidity and control. They feel their energy being sucked out of them every time they turn around; their internal flame keeps dying out. They almost get there, they almost make it, and then something goes wrong — their physical health suffers, their finances suffer, the kids get in trouble, and they have problems at work.

Addictions rip them and their families apart, they feel responsible for everything, they live from crisis to crisis, they care so deeply for others that they don't care for themselves, and the list goes on and on.

The first community is the New Age/Metaphysical community. The New Age/Metaphysical community consists of churches large and small, psychic healers, psychics, mediums, body workers, therapists, wellness facilitators, channeler's and its own share of quacks. Most of the metaphysical churches tell us that God is a God of love, not rear. Most try to stay away from sexist language. "Our Creator" is an oft-used term. They teach what we hold to be true will come true. If you believe in lack; in shortages; you will experience lack and shortages. If you believe in illness, you will experience illness and so on and so on. They believe that there is a wonderful magical light in the universe and if you believe and practice certain exercises, you can bask in this light. Others believe that the light is internal, that it resides within you, and by following directions or suggestions you can radiate this light. I think they are both right.

There is the internal light that we are born with that often doesn't make it through the first five years of our life without someone shutting it off. And there is the eternal light of the universe that we were born into and intended to bathe in. Many people in (and out of) the New Age/Metaphysical community work hard to stamp out social injustice. They devote time and money to protecting Mother Earth. They work to bring an end to nuclear weapons and war. They do what they can for the homeless. They understand that we human beings were designed to need help and to give each other a hand. Some believe they are here to give help and don't need help.

Whatever the situation, I have seen too many doing wonderful works but having no sense of self, no life of their own. Jesus did the cross. I don't think we are supposed to continue on year after year hanging ourselves on it. The day of the cross was a day of darkness. Standing in the light and casting a shadow is about being present in your body, about a sense of self. It's about our feelings, this aspect of our humanness that we use denial, alcohol, drugs, food, sex, money, activity, relationships, work, and many other things to escape. Without the feelings, there is no self. Without a self there is no shadow. We are incomplete.

The other is the recovery community. For the most part the recovery community consists of two phases. The first phase involves recovering from addictions: alcohol, drugs, food, gambling, spending, sex, love, money, work, service. The second phase involves recovering from the results of having been raised in some type of dysfunctional family. This group is in private therapy, group therapy, Adult Children of Alcoholics Anonymous (ACoA/ ACA), Codependency Anonymous (CODA), Incest Survivors Anonymous (ISA) and others. Many have been through some type of inpatient treatment.

There are cross-over members in both communities and in both phases of recovery. Some have gotten into recovery from addictions by way of the New Age community, others have gotten into metaphysics through recovery, and still others have gotten into addiction recovery through ACA, CODA, or ISA.

Having spent half of my life in one community or the other and having experienced all of the frustrations listed above, I have come to see that the answer is a partnership between the principles of both communities. Without this partnership most people will stay stuck at some level of their progress. They will fall short of their dreams. They will run out of energy before the adventure is half over.

You may be reading this and saying that you have never cracked the cover of a New Age or metaphysical book, that you have never gone to a metaphysical church or a psychic or had your tarot cards read, or that you don't belong to any twelve-step recovery program. Is there anything in this book for you?

If you feel like your life is on hold, like you're stuck, you're missing something, you wish it were over, that there is a secret out there that other people know but no one told you, that three minutes before you die you're going to realize you missed it all, that there's something wrong with you, that you're insufficient, inadequate, that happiness is for frivolous people, that duty is everything, being in control is essential, like you must have something to hate to exist, that love means what are you going to do for me — then this book is absolutely for you.

AUTHOR'S NOTE

SOMEONE ONCE SAID A BOOK IS MEANT to be a
battleground of ideas. When you finish this book, if it is marked
up, ripped, bent and generally mangled I will take it as the
highest compliment. I know most of you find the thought of
defacing (I'll use your word) anything unthinkable.

Do me a favor. Go buy a couple of highlighters, preferably
yellow and red. Highlight everything you like in yellow and
everything you don't like in red. If you have an opposing
opinion write it in the margin, or on the pages provided in the
back of the book. Challenge this book like I am going to
challenge your B.S. belief system, that is.

In these pages I hope you will go to war with me, make up
with me, cry with me, laugh with me, get mad with me and at
me, and in the end respect us both for having the courage to
experience the adventure of getting acquainted with our
human-being, turning on the inner light and stepping into the
light of the universe.

CONTENTS

WHO TURNED OUT THE LIGHT?

The people blinded by its brilliance.

I ARRIVED ON THIS PLANET BUTT-FIRST with a full set of feelings. I believe that these feelings are an integral part of the life experience I am meant to have. I am a human being, and I am here to have the human experience... which includes feelings. When I am cut off from my feelings there is no me. I am not in my body, I do not exist, and no matter how much light there is, I do not cast a shadow... My internal light was turned out a long, long time ago.

When I am cut off from myself I do not know how to function with others in the healthy inter-dependence that is necessary for the survival of the human race. My relationships were obsessive, compulsive, desperate, co-dependent.

From age twelve to age forty-five, a type of smile caused me no end of pain. The smile usually came from a female. I paid for more attention to smiles from girls and women than I did from men. These smiles would come from a female who was in touch with her feelings, had a full supply of self-esteem, and was a true, free spirit. At first the smile was like a powerful magnet, a

1

mysterious attraction, a barker in the carnival of light calling me to come and experience the magic of his sideshow, the enchanted forest, and the secret of life. That initial reaction would last for three seconds and then I would become aware of my own darkness, my own burned out light. I felt flawed. I didn't know my light had only been turned out.

Something in me had connected with the light in the other person, and for a few seconds I felt magic. There was something familiar about the light although I had no conscious memory of my own light. The energy about these women was at the same time seductive in a spiritual sense and frightening on an emotional level. Because of where I was in my own life, I usually interpreted the seduction as physical, sexual, not spiritual. Something in me connected with the energy, some vague faraway memory, some far away voice calling to me, quickly silenced by the belief that my energy generators were inoperable – also flawed, damaged, broken, or missing.

So I wandered through life with beautiful, open people acknowledging me with genuine smiles, but it was grinding me up on the inside. I came to prefer insincere smiles.

Children are born on this planet with three-hundred-sixty degrees of energy and reflecting the light of the universe at all who come near. I am the fifty-five-year-old father of a three-and-a-half-year-old daughter and know this to be true. In a nurturing environment, children's energy is honored and the parents and child all bathe in the light.

Unfortunately for most of us, this is not usually the case. Everything in my early life: was about turning out the light and shutting off the energy. I didn't know this on a conscious level as I had no childhood memories. After eight years of intensive therapy, twenty years of metaphysical work and twenty-nine years in recovery from alcoholism and drug addiction, I was finally able to put the pieces together.

I was born to parents who probably shouldn't have had a child. Their primary concern was "not making waves in life" and "making sure that others thought well of them". This meant that their child — me — had to be "seen and not heard!" This is another way of "turning out the light" and putting a lid on that energy. My mother accomplished this with her fists and my father with his silence. My mother kept her own light out and her energy squashed by focusing all of her attention on others. My father used alcohol.

By the time I started school I was using most of my energy to keep my light from showing through the cracks and the energy of the universe from setting me on fire. I didn't have much left fur school work. According to today's system, I suffered from an attention deficit. In those days, I was just considered dumb. Many children who come out of stress-filled homes suffer from attention deficit. The goings-on at home eat up their life energy.

I know now that a constant turmoil went on inside me. I wanted to run and shout and scream and play and sing and be silly. I wanted to bathe in and reflect the light of the universe. But — and this is a very big BUT — the need to survive was stronger. To survive I had to turn out any light that blinded my parents and contain any energy that made them uncomfortable. When I hit the school system, I had to pull in most of my remaining energy and walk in darkness.

By the time I was fifteen, the school system no longer wanted me.... This was mutual. I was bored to tears and somewhere deep inside I knew I wasn't dumb. I just didn't think I was smart. My energy cried out to be released and my being cried out for light. Someone gave me a funny-looking cigarette

3

and said smoke this. I did and suddenly I didn't feel so flawed. A little light shone through and my stomach became as hungry as my soul.

That was the beginning of an eleven-year run of drugs, alcohol and sex, which was my attempt to stop the pain and find the light. It was an eleven-year run to find whatever it was that my being was crying out for. It was an eleven-year run at feeling inferior and trying to cover it up with drugs and alcohol.

The price that period of my life extracted was terrible. Lost jobs, adultery, tears, beatings given, beatings received, jail, lies, serious auto accidents, an addled brain, a dark cavern within and a shriveled soul. Oh sure, I had a few brief periods of looking good on the outside (my mother was proud) but that didn't slow the destruction on the inside. I was lost and alone in a crowd. The only light was coming from police spotlights, mug shot cameras and an occasional internal flash of light from having put together some bizarre, abstract combination of chemicals. The voice crying out for unification of my human being and spirit, for light, for connection with the energy of the universe was dead... almost.

My wife just arrived home from the humane shelter with two black kittens. Our daughter is so excited she can't stand still. Our last two cats disappeared into the desert. I assume they became part of the food chain. This should be quite wonderful watching Sasha's adventures with the kittens.

They appear to be strong enough to survive the enthusiasm of a child. I will of course help that cause.

At twenty-six years of age I was living in doorways. My life was over. I wanted to die and didn't have the energy left to do it. I thought about throwing a brick through a liquor store window, taking the booze and sitting down and having a drink

4

until they came to take me to jail. Then suddenly an Eskimo came along and my life was about to take a major turn for the better. I need to go forward in time to explain what an Eskimo is. Eskimos are an indication that light and energy still exist, that a power in the universe is still at work in people's lives. I couldn't see this at the time, but then it was hard being in touch with what was going on in my life when I was so seldom present in my body... which was 99 percent of the time. Let me explain Eskimos.

When I had been off the drugs and alcohol for about two years I was having great difficulty with a concept of God that would give me hope. All I could envision when someone said God was the old man in the sky, sitting in a throne with a large book in his lap, keeping score. People in the recovery fellowship were telling me God was within me, God loved me, God would help me. But I knew if God was good then God wasn't inside me because I was flawed, inadequate, insufficient, dark and disconnected from the universe and no God worth His or Her salt would hang out in a sewer.

God might help people in the sewer but He wouldn't hang out there. Also, if God were keeping score, I wasn't anywhere close to being even. When I would go to pray, my mind would say to me "Forget it, God only helps the good guys and you're not one of the good guys." It has been said that it is common for those of us who grew up in a dysfunctional environment as children that our God will closely resemble one of our parents or primary care givers. No wonder I wasn't rushing to establish a relationship with this God.

Anyway, one night I was sitting in a meeting of the fellowship worried about God and what to do when I heard the speaker tell the following story. Since then I have talked to others who were at the same meeting and they didn't hear the story, so you can draw your own conclusions as to how I heard it or where it came from.

Two men were drinking in a bar in Alaska. One was an extremely religious man, the other an atheist. The Atheist said, "I don't believe in your God?' The Religious man asked, "Why not?" The Atheist said that once not long ago he had given God a chance to prove Himself and God failed. The Religious man asked in what manner had the Atheist given God a chance to prove himself. The Atheist said three months before he had been lost fifty miles north of town in a blizzard. He had knelt down in the blowing snow and screamed, "God if you're there I'm lost and I'm going to die." The Religious man looked at the Atheist and smiled a knowing smile and said, "You must believe...you're here?' The Atheist said, "No, an Eskimo came along and showed me the way back to town."

Well, the Eskimo standing over me in my doorway was a guy who owed me some money and between a sense of responsibility and his good heart, he offered to let me come stay with him and his wife.

That night, in a one-bedroom apartment with him, his wife and their eight children, I mentioned that I was going to have to do something about my drinking and drugging.

He told me there was a girl down the hall in recovery from alcoholism. The year was 1962 and I was curious to see what a girl recovering from alcoholism looked like.

I went down the hall, knocked on the door and a girl big enough to break every bone in my body opened it. She stood about six foot two, weighed two-hundred-thirty pounds and had tattoos up and down both arms and both legs. She had a half-full pint of alcohol in one hand. Now a lot of people might not consider this a good introduction to alcohol recovery but she was the perfect Eskimo for me.

I told her I was curious about recovery and she said it would work if wanted it and she wasn't ready to quit drinking. That made perfect sense to me. She was big and strong. If were still big and strong I wouldn't quit either but I wasn't.... I was at the end of the line and had shoved the train a few feet further. She stuck me in her car and took me to a meeting of the fellowship to which she belonged, and I haven't found it necessary to use mind-altering chemicals of any kind since. I was headed back into the light. My internal light had begun to flicker ever so slightly, like a candle in the wind and a pin-point of light had begun to shine down on me.

.

2

A MATCH IS STRUCK

A little light for me.
A little light for others.

WHEN MY ESKIMO TOOK ME to my first meeting of twelve-step recovery from alcohol and drugs, my inner light began to shine ever so slightly. People said they understood, they cared. They said come back. If you don't have a car we will get you a ride. They told stories about the pain and suffering of alcohol and drug addiction that I could identify with and laugh at. Early on the laughter healed me, but years later when I was still laughing at the same incidents from my past, I was driving an emotional nail into my coffin.

What had happened was interesting, tragic. I was no longer being washed under by drugs and alcohol. I was about to drown in recovery.

In the beginning people picked me up in their cars and took me to meetings of the fellowship. After meetings a group would go out for coffee and they took me along. Sometimes we went to someone's house. Sometimes we went to a coffee shop.

I had nowhere to live, and two members allowed me to stay at their house in exchange for painting a little one-bedroom, wood-frame house next door that they rented out. It took me ten days to paint that little house. I was not in the best of shape, so it was constantly a mystery to me why people would spend time with me and help me. With each of these encounters, the light inside me would glow a little brighter. The hope burners had been ignited.

After a while I had a job and a car, and I was taking people to meetings and coffee. When I had been sober a year, some members took me to a meeting of an institutional panel where if you were accepted, you were given the opportunity to carry the light to those in prison, jail, or hospitals. I was accepted and another means of giving back what had been given to me was in place.

By the time I was two years off alcohol and drugs I was busy taking people to meetings, putting meetings on in institutions, taking people to coffee and sponsoring people. To be a sponsor meant the opportunity to answer questions, provide transportation when needed and help the person with the twelve steps.

Belle is dead. Hit by a car today. Tina and I held each other and cried over the loss of the youngest of our three dogs. She filled the house with her spirit, her antics. I looked into my wife's eyes when we finished the first round of crying. It had been a while since I have seen the incredible beauty that lives inside her. Does a dog have to die for me to take the time to see my wife's inner beauty? No, sometimes it just seems that way.

We went to Sabino Canyon to say good-bye to Belle. We were never able to bring her here. No pets allowed. God, how Belle would have loved to run these canyons. She loved to run more than anything in the world except perhaps a tie with stealing food. A red Dobie with floppy ears — those ears would fold back on top of her head when she ran. She had the constitution of a Chesapeake. She would go straight through a barbed wire fence after a rabbit and not even flinch. We thought she was indestructible.

From a small overlook I raised my hat, my favorite hat, to the saguaros, the mountains, the stream, the clouds, the sky — goodbye Belle. May your spirit run at my side throughout my life forever. Walking back down from the overlook we whistled good-bye to her. We whistled the sounds that we had used to call her. She didn't come... but then she didn't come half of the time when she was alive. Thank you for sharing this moment of pain and loss with me. Loss is a terrible thing but to not be able to experience it is worse.

What follow are the twelve steps as printed in the "Big Book" of Alcoholics Anonymous.

1. We admitted we were powerless over alcohol — that our lives had become unmanageable.

2. Came to believe that a Power greater than ourselves could restore us to sanity.

3. Made a decision to turn our will and our lives over to the care of God as we understood Him.

4. Made a searching and fearless moral inventory of ourselves.

5. Admitted to God, to ourselves and to another human being the exact nature of our wrongs.

6. Were entirely ready to have God remove all these defects of character.

7. Humbly asked Him to remove our shortcomings.

8. Made a list of all persons we had harmed, and became willing to make amends to them all.

9. Made direct amends to such people wherever possible, except when to do so would injure them or others.

10. Continued to take personal inventory and when we were wrong promptly admitted it.

11. Sought through prayer and meditation to improve our conscious contact with God as we understood Him, praying only for knowledge of His will for us and the power to carry that out.

12. Having had a spiritual awakening as the result of these steps, we tried to carry this message to alcoholics, and to practice these principles in all our affairs.

In the introduction I listed some of the programs that are currently using the twelve steps. As a rule, about the only thing different groups change in the steps is whatever the specific group is powerless over.

Twelve-step recovery began with Alcoholics Anonymous back in the 1930s. It all started with one alcoholic taking the time to talk to another alcoholic and together they were able to stay sober. Eventually there were a hundred of them, and they put together the twelve steps and wrote a book.

At first the steps were an absolute mystery to me. The part that made sense was that if I could get free from the addiction there would have to be a God or someone with a hell of a lot more power than I had. On the other hand, because at the core of my being I felt flawed, less than, insufficient, terminally ill, I doubted that a God would help me. But people said time after time, "Keep coming to meetings and it will be okay."

I staggered in, in darkness, and the people in twelve-step recovery handed me the first light I had had in a very long time that wasn't chemically induced. When I got stronger I passed the light on to others and they passed it on to others. I learned two important lessons in recovery. Early on, the smallest of problems could overwhelm me, and I was quickly taught to "Turn it over."

"Turn it over" meant stop worrying about it, stop obsessing about it, surrender it to God and go on with your life. Based on watching those around me at the time, it also meant stuff any feelings you may have on the subject and move on down the road. Don't get angry. Don't get sad. "Turn it over."

The second lesson I learned early on was "When all else fails, work with an alcoholic who is still suffering." Based on watching those around me, this meant forget yourself, forget your feelings, forget your needs and focus all your attention on somebody else's needs.

Now in the early stages of my recovery, these slogans saved my life. I could get completely crazy over an envelope from an agency or person from my past without even opening the envelope to see what was inside. Like many alcoholics, I had a past filled with unresolved situations that were snapping at my heels like a fire-breathing dragon... money owed, lies told, actions taken or not taken, and so forth.

So being able to throw these things to this unseen God, or hurl myself into concentrating on others, kept me from going completely berserk. A great many of the issues resolved themselves. When I stopped myself from creating so much anxiety that I was paralyzed, I was able to do something constructive about those that did not resolve themselves.

The interesting and tragic element in all of this is that the very beliefs that got me through some of the roughest times were to eventually become mirrors in my emotional house of horror, hiding from me the feelings that I so desperately needed on the one hand and was so violently afraid of on the other hand. My feelings are my connection with my humanness.

All the feelings I had repressed since a child seemed like a strong wind threatening to blow out the match. It scared the hell out of me. I had no tools, no skills to protect the match, block the wind. Each time I felt the match threatened I would "turn it over" or "work with others." It got to a point where I was sponsoring fifty people. The telephone calls alone consumed a third of my twenty-four hours. I still felt like I was going under and I wasn't doing enough. What I didn't understand was the match didn't need protection from the feelings.

A real fear among many in recovery is that feelings — both present and past — will lead them to relapse, and will return them to their addiction. Perhaps in some cases that might be true, I don't know. I do know that for those like myself who used their addiction as one more means of controlling, stuffing, hiding from their feelings, hiding from themselves — that continuing to run from, stuff or otherwise avoid their feelings can lead to an explosion that guarantees relapse.

Eventually the pain becomes so great that they will be left with no choice but to return to what once worked. When I use the word "explosion," I mean sometimes external explosion but always internal explosion. Sometimes nothing big or dramatic shows up on the exterior of the person... He or she just goes quietly away and resumes the addiction... some come back... most do not.

Today, many treatment centers and programs move the brand-new recovering addict, alcoholic, bulimic, anorexic or overeater into their feelings in the very beginning of their recovery. It is sort of an introduction to the person they are and the feelings they've been running from while they are still slightly numb. Those I have talked with who are running these programs are convinced that it greatly reduces the chances for relapse. Time will tell. They believe that continuing to remain estranged from oneself in recovery can only lead to misery.

That was my experience. By the time I was seventeen years off drugs and alcohol I was ready for a padded room somewhere and a class in basket-weaving. "Turning it over" no longer worked. I had begun to hate the people I was working with. I felt ripped off every time I spent time with them.

You see, spending time with them no longer stopped my pain.

Now there are plenty of people in this society who lose themselves in their family and friends with the same results. Early on in their life this works, but as the years roll by, they begin to secretly resent the very same people they are giving their lives to. Other people will lose themselves in their work or hobbies or affairs or hide in their mind through compulsive thinking or stuffing it full of useless information. They begin to resent whatever their choice of escape has been.

Eventually, the light inside us that was dimmed in childhood begins to cry and then scream to be set free. But even the thought of giving up our choice of escape sends terror through us. In many ways those of us who are addicts and alcoholics are fortunate. The choice we made to hide from and control our feelings brings us to our knees in front of the executioner where the only chance we have is to give up our primary means of escape or die.

Many people who have lost themselves in their work, or in others, have taken their own lives when they reach that point of realizing they have no tools for using the match to light the candle. But a much larger number go to their grave finding additional ways to ignore the internal cry for help. With the practicing alcoholic and addict (including people with eating disorders), there is a guaranteed early death, imprisonment or psychiatric hospitalization.

Feelings are the oxygen the match needs to burn brighter and light the candle.

3

THE MATCH MEETS THE CANDLE

If I can just keep from blowing it out.

THE INITIAL YEARS OF RECOVERY were primarily devoted to not drinking, not using drugs, working with others and cleaning up some of the mess I had made during the previous eleven years. After a couple years, my yearning for light and energy became stronger. I didn't understand it so I drowned it in cigarettes, coffee, sugar and sex. But it wasn't to be denied. By the time I was seven or eight years off drugs and alcohol I began to actively seek the light... Self Realization Fellowship, Infinity Way (Joel Goldsmith), T.M., Emmet Fox, Unity, the list goes on.

In retrospect, it was a fascinating time. Actually, it wasn't dull when I was going through it. I remember grabbing onto a line somewhere that said, "See the God in everyone, look in their eyes and see their beauty." Suddenly I found myself having sex with women that prior to that time I wouldn't have found attractive. Perhaps to some extent I missed the message.

Now I was thirty-four years old and eight years off drugs and alcohol, and I had found another tool to cut me off from me. I had found meditation — meditation that took me out of myself. The yardstick for how good a student you were was how far out of yourself you got and how long you stayed there. I was a great student. I had been getting out of myself since I was two years old. Staying inside myself, being present in my body and in my life, was my problem. Although I strolled down the New Age/Metaphysical path with light coming from all sides, I didn't cast a shadow. No one was home. And one of the reasons no one was home was that it still hurt like hell to be in there.

I adopted an enlightened personality in an attempt to hide my pain from myself and others. I knew how to pray, meditate, affirm, visualize and channel. I spoke enlightenment. My words and performance (my failure) made it impossible for anybody to draw attention to the pain and emptiness in my eyes. I didn't spend time around people who could see through me. I hadn't lost the feeling of being inferior, flawed, and insufficient. In the last few years I have met some folks that use colored contact lenses to give their eyes a look of wellness, enlightenment, strength. The lengths we go to in order to hide our pain from ourselves and others are limited only by our imagination.

Thank God for the two black kittens. They have made Belle's loss easier for Sasha. She had been completely occupied with them for the last few days. She hasn't been looking for Belle to dress or decorate with stickers.

However, tonight at dinner she asked where Belle was. We told her she had run into the road, been hit by a car and wasn't coming home again ever. We sat quietly while she worked that out. After about a minute and a half of silence she said, — Weren't there two Belles and couldn't we get the other one?" Tina and I said, "Yes, there were, and yes, we could." New kittens, a new dog to come soon... life goes barking and meowing on.

When I was embracing enlightenment in those days I was trying to accomplish two things — to achieve what I knew at some level was spiritually possible — while at the same time continuing to cut myself off from my feelings. My spiritual successes were partial or short-lived. The feelings kept trying to get loose. Not having experienced feelings since I was a small child I interpreted these unruly feelings that were trying to get free as mental illness. I thought I was losing my mind.

The pain was increasing, and although I was off hard drugs and alcohol, I still had plenty of chemicals to choose from. I smoked more cigarettes, drank more coffee, ate more sugar, shoveled in more grease and salt, looked for more women to sleep with, spent more time lost in sexual or romantic fantasies and watched more television. I was writing for television at the time so I had a built-in excuse to watch television. I still had a sense of the light, but I couldn't confirm it because there was no shadow. I was, however, reflecting a flickering inner light to many in recovery.

Although I could meditate hours at a time (and experienced the "thunder of silence"), the moment I was finished I wanted a cigarette and sex. And somewhere between thirty and forty minutes after meditating, an elusive anger would begin to roam around inside me like a prowler in the fog. I realize now it was a combination of my inner self being angry that I had found one more way to disconnect, coupled with all the unexpressed anger stored since childhood.

This anger would then unload at the first opportunity on some poor clerk or someone in traffic or a family member. So I would finish an hour or so of meditation, emerge refreshed and standing in the light, and in thirty minutes be chasing some guy through traffic at ninety miles an hour giving him the finger and screaming obscenities. The frightening thing about all this was not my chasing some guy through traffic... it was that I didn't see anything wrong. Yes, I was expressing anger but not appropriately. When one or more lives are being put at risk, it is definitely not appropriate.

Metaphysics wasn't providing me with tools to express my anger. I was being told to look at myself, be understanding of others and turn the other cheek. Healthy limits and boundaries are critical to emotional well-being, but if I can't have my anger, I don't know where to set my boundaries.

I had moved into the world of the spirit, found relief briefly, followed by more confusion.

Just as I would change a drug when it no longer gave me what I was looking for, I slowly began to let slide any metaphysical work. How could I feel so terrible? Hadn't I meditated, prayed, opened my chakras, channeled my higher self, thrown enough tarot cards to supply Las Vegas bathed in the light? What the hell had gone wrong?

I would find moments of spiritual bliss only to have them disappear in a blast of low self-esteem. I was at war with ghosts I didn't know existed and I wasn't present in my body to fight the war. As Scott Peck said in The Road Less Traveled, "Life is difficult". True... but it isn't meant to be a struggle. I was struggling, and the New Age/Metaphysical tools weren't the first I had used to continue the separation from self.

When I hit the wall at seventeen years sober, I had no idea what was wrong with me. I didn't know where to go. I didn't know what to do. "Turn it over" and "work with others" were threatening to blow out the match. They had become cracks in the windbreak. What had saved my life in the beginning had ceased to work for me. Many people in twelve-step recovery use these principles for their entire lives. They never return to their primary addiction and say they are quite happy. I, on the other hand, could feel the candle going out.

I want to add a little story here. At this point I am in the process of going over the manuscript of this book and making the changes and additions (that appeal to me) suggested by Susan Newcomer, my more than wonderful editor. She has also done all of what would normally be a copy editor's work: the commas, spelling, correct phrasing, etc. Now I hate making the copy editor's changes. This is left-brain work that drives me crazy. I practically stop breathing, my shoulders and neck get stiff and I will do anything to avoid sitting down and doing the work. In fact this morning my wife said to me that reading the livestock sales was carrying my resisting a little too far. Yesterday when it was time to start making the changes I lay down on my office floor, stomped my feet, beat my fists and screamed "I don't want to do the changes, I hate doing changes." I went at it for five minutes or so.

I know people in both the recovery and New Age/Metaphysical communities that would be appalled at that behavior. I would be expected to tell myself how blessed I was that I had a second book that was going to be published. How obvious it was that God loved me. How I should count my blessings and stop whining. How many people out there would willingly

*change places with me and do the changes
with a smile on their face?*

*What those well-meaning people who would
try to stop me from what they believe to be
suffering don't understand is: I KNOW ALL OF
THAT! But telling myself how blessed I am
before I express my true feelings over what is
going on is nothing more than another method
to repress the feelings, shove the human into
the closet and pretend things are wonderful.
This is one more way to blow out my own
candle.*

*I am thrilled to have a second book that is
going to be published. I know God loves me. I
still hate doing the copy editor's changes yet
God still loves me.*

4

THE LIGHT AT THE END OF THE TUNNEL IS A TRAIN

*My life was rocketing down the tracks
and I wasn't on board.*

I WAS EITHER ON A SIDING, IN A STATION, or tied to the tracks. Although light is the subject, my life often felt like a runaway train. I kept looking for a Conductor to tell me what was going on.

Obviously there was an Engineer, a God. I was seventeen years off drugs and alcohol and I was a successful television writer. But where the hell was the Conductor, the person with the flashlight to help me read my ticket and tell me where the train was going, what were the stations, how much was the fare, why I didn't feel like I belonged on my train?

All I had to do was reflect on how I came to be a successful television writer to know there was a kind and gentle Engineer driving the train.

When I was four years off drugs and alcohol things weren't going remarkably well by my reckoning. I had gone bankrupt to clear up the financial wreckage of my drinking. I had returned my car to the finance company. I was sleeping on the sofa of a guy I didn't particularly like but he lived next door to the car wash I was working at. I was earning $1.25 an hour. I had started at $1.35 in the soap end but I got a rash from the detergents and had to be moved to the dry-off end. Bouncing in and out off hot car seats all day reactivated the hemorrhoids I had gotten over the years from sitting on concrete jail floors. I hadn't been with a woman in five months. Needless to say I didn't feel the ever-present energy of a Kind and Loving Power in my life. And the only time I cast a shadow was when someone would give me a quarter tip (it would buy a pack of cigarettes) for drying off his or her car. For a moment I felt validated.

One day an Eskimo drove through the car wash and offered me a better job. It seemed to me like it had been a long time since I had seen an Eskimo. But then again I'm sure more than a few had slipped through my life unnoticed.

The Eskimo who drove through the car wash asked me what I was doing working in a car wash and I told him I didn't know. He said he could give me a job as a trim press operator in a die-casting company that was two blocks away and paid fifty cents more an hour... Yahoo! A gift from God... more money and close enough to walk... I took the job. After a couple of weeks they trained me to be a die-caster instead of a trim press operator... and more money. It wasn't long before I could afford my own little apartment nearby. I couldn't afford a car but I was making enough money to begin to pay off some of the people I had gone bankrupt on. Soon a woman appeared on the horizon. She had three great children, a car and a house. I kept my apartment but we spent a good deal of time together.

A year went by after my encounter with the Eskimo. I had a job, apartment, and woman. I wanted to die. On the outside things were better, but on the inside things hadn't changed. I was still smoking tons of cigarettes, eating pounds of sugar, drinking gallons of coffee, watching lots of television, having lots of sexual fantasies, just a myriad of addictions still going which kept me from my feelings. Finally one night in desperation I looked at the ceiling in my apartment and screamed to God, "If you're not there, I'm fucked." (The prayer may offend some of you, but if your life is in such a state that one word can destroy the power of a moment, I suggest you read on.) I knew if there were no God, I was finished. I had done the best job I could and I was miserable.

The next day I walked to work and nothing had changed. Later that day at work I placed a brand new wrench into a brand new bolt (they were machined for each other). The wrench slipped, I fell backwards and crushed two vertebrae in my back. A short time later, lying in the cubicle at the emergency hospital, I was told I couldn't return to that line of work. I couldn't stand for long periods of time and couldn't lift.

My back was in bad shape before this accident. When the doctors walked out of the cubicle and my mind immediately launched into an assault on me about how I finally surrendered to God and He broke my back. I was too whipped to listen and told my mind to stuff it. I decided that who knows, maybe breaking my back was a good deal. I was sick and tired of analyzing, figuring, scheming, worrying, projecting disaster. I was tired of compulsive thinking. I left the hospital and went about simply doing what was put in front of me to do. I filed for vocational rehabilitation, went for physical therapy, and collected my disability payments.

Vocational rehabilitation didn't know what to do with me. I didn't have a high school diploma (I had been thrown out). I didn't have a trade. Every time they would give me an aptitude test, I would come out something different. I wasn't being a smart-ass. For the first time in my life I was answering the questions based on how I felt that day. Not how I thought I should answer them or how I thought they wanted me to answer them. After six months Voc rehab hadn't been able to come up with anything we could agree on.

Then one night I was sitting in my apartment reading T. V. Guide (what else?) and I saw an ad for a writing school in Westport, Connecticut. A little voice inside me said, "Let's try that." There was no intellectual rationale for this decision. I had failed every English class I had ever taken. I was thrown out of high school in the tenth grade. I was a phonetic speller and didn't know anything about writing.

Two and a half years earlier I had carried a tablet and a pencil to MacArthur Park in Los Angeles and sat down to write the great American novel. It took me about ten minutes to talk myself out of that one. I took the tablet and pencil home and put them away. No one else in my life has ever hated me enough to put in the time and energy that I have put in talking myself out of wondrous adventures.

Sasha just announced that she is getting too big for her potty and we will have to give it away soon. A couple of months ago she was "too big" far her crib and now she has a big girl bed. The crib has been given to a shelter for another child to use. Our daughter approves of that. One time when John James and I were doing a workshop in Los Angeles on grief a woman was in terrible distress: she had come home from pre-school and her parents had given her high-chair away. This can be a big time betrayal to a child. Thank God for family of origin recovery... Sasha gets to tell us when she is ready. Her power and energy remain intact. (most of the time)

I took the ad in to my voc rehab counselor. She laughed so hard she almost fell out of her chair. She too, knew all the reasons why it was silly... but she took the ad into her boss. Because I had been on their rolls so long, he would have agreed to pay for basket-weaving school to get rid of me. They agreed to pay for the course. Many times the main ingredient in "letting go" is patience. We have to wait until all of the players are in place and we are ready before we go forward.

I applied to the school and they sent me a sample picture from which to compose a five-hundred word story. I wrote it and sent it in. Obviously I passed because a salesman soon called. I'm not sure everyone who wrote in didn't pass — but at the time it didn't matter. He signed me up and left me half a dozen copies of a monthly magazine the school put out. In the magazine was a section called "Student Sales," which contained letters from students who had sold their very first piece. They had sold some to their church paper, some to magazines, some to publishers. No matter what they had written they had sold something. Somebody had paid them for their writing, and they were just "folks" carpenters, housewives, retired people, cab drivers, just "folks" — which meant there was hope for me.

The woman I was seeing had been married to a composer, and so she and the children were highly supportive of anything creative. They were terrific.

Soon my books came and I did my first assignment and sent it in. While I was waiting for a reply, I tried writing a short story. It was awful. I read further on in my books. They said it is important for first time writers to write for media they are familiar with. Well, I hadn't read many books or short stories but I had watched an obsessive amount of television. I tried writing a story for "Bonanza." It was on a par with my short story. The idea was okay (I later did it for "The Virginian") but

27

the execution left a little to be desired. I kept reading in my books. They said not only is it important to write for a medium that you are familiar with — it is important to write about what you know.

I knew what I didn't know. I didn't know the old West. What I did know was a little about crime from my days as a juvenile delinquent (this lasted till I was 26). I started watching the cop shows on television. Finally I settled on "Ironside". I liked the show. Ironside had difficult crimes to solve. I sat down and tried to think of a situation I hadn't seen on television. Finally I settled on doing a story about a paperhanger. Not a wallpaper installer but someone who cashes bad payroll checks. Having done this once, I felt qualified to write about it. Now I was writing for a medium I was familiar with and writing about something I knew about! Yet, still felt lost. I went ahead and started to write the story anyway.

About a week later I encountered another Eskimo. I was at a meeting of the fellowship I belonged to and one of the guys, Jim, offered me a ride home (I still didn't have a car). On the way home he asked me what I did. Now, I had no idea what Jim did. I had made a point of not knowing what people in this organization did for a living. I was there to stay off drugs and alcohol. Although I would tell you otherwise, I knew I was easily influenced by people's positions. So I didn't want to find myself giving help to one person over another because of what they did. I told Jim I was writing a story for television. He said, "Oh really. That's great. That's what I do."

"What do you do?" I asked.

"I write for television and if you want any help or would like me to take a look at what you've done, I'd be glad to."

Suddenly I didn't feel so lost. I knew an Eskimo when I saw one. I gave him my story. He had a dozen suggestions. The half dozen I liked I made. The other half dozen I ignored. I was exercising creative choice and didn't even know it.

A week later, when I had finished the changes, he said if I wanted to have someone type up a finished copy, he knew a girl that belonged to the same fellowship that we did who did typing in the evening to make extra money. You bet I needed someone to type up a finished copy. I don't think Universal Studios knew that "dead" was spelled "ded."

Enter the next Eskimo. This one was named Carol. I dropped the story off at her house and she said she would have it finished in a couple of days. I spent the next two days wondering how the hell I was going to get the story into the studio where someone would read it. I still didn't know Carol was an Eskimo.

Two nights later, true to her word, Carol called and said she had finished typing the story. Not only had she finished typing it — she had read it and really liked it. I was on cloud nine. Then she asked me if Jim had told me where she worked. I told her no. She informed me that she was secretary to the associate producer of "Ironside" and if I would like, she would take my story in for him to read. I was thrilled. A real dilemma had been resolved. She took it in. I was wandering in a forest with no map. But through the simple act of believing that everything was going to work out like it was supposed to it did.

I wasn't afraid to go through the open doors because I didn't have any choice. The associate producer read it, liked it and passed it on to the executive producer. The executive producer called me in for a meeting. I called my friend Jim and said, "What do I do now? I have never been to a studio. I don't know what to do." He told me not to worry and that everything would be okay. He told me that although the Writers Guild forbids the executive producer from asking me to make any changes unless he was willing to pay for them that I should do whatever the executive producer asked. That made sense to me.

Two days later I stood looking up at that ominous black tower at Universal Studios. On the way up in the elevator I said to God (who I still wasn't sure was animal, vegetable, mineral or spirit) that if He didn't get off the elevator with me, I was in deep trouble.

I located the executive producer's office. Just as I informed Karen, his secretary (who was to become a good friend) that I was there, I could hear this man in the inner office screaming at a telephone repair man. I thought, "Oh-oh." Karen quietly informed me that she was new working for him but understood that he screamed a lot and not to worry about it. I didn't relax.

Once in his office I liked him a lot. He was a straight shooter ... no bullshit. He liked the story but he didn't like the way Ironside figured out how to catch the guy passing the bad checks. I had Ironside figure out the guy's pattern, get ahead of him, and arrest him. The executive producer informed me that the plaque on the back of Ironside's wheelchair said "The Greatest Detective in the World," and any cop could do what Ironside had done in my story. I agreed to go home and find a better way.

Now this is where going through open doors and writing about what I knew first-hand really came in handy. I sat down at home and thought, okay, what kind of a problem did my two partners and I have when we were passing bad checks (payroll checks we had printed against non-existent companies)? The answer came immediately — groceries. We would go through the check-out stand of a super market to cash the checks because in those days, if you had a basket full of groceries they wouldn't scrutinize the checks as closely.

Well, we were passing three to six checks a day apiece. We had groceries coming out of our ears. We located every girl or guy we had known in high school who had gotten married and didn't have any money and we would drop off $200 worth of groceries, which in 1953 amounted to twenty or so bags. I was taking ten to twenty bags of groceries home every night.

My mother (my parents were divorced) who was parenting by the 'hear no evil, see no evil' method, never said a word when she would open a cupboard and find twenty canned hams or thirty-five bottles of ketchup. I decided that my character in the story didn't have any friends he could give the groceries to, so he was dumping them in a dumpster behind a deserted Y.M.C.A.

Going through a pile of the bad checks, Ironside takes note of the amount of groceries being purchased (the checker writes it on the check) and starts to go to the garbage collection companies to see if any of them have found new groceries in any of the dumpsters. When he arrives at one of the companies, the employees are dividing up the goodies. Reluctantly, they tell Ironside where the dumpster is and Ironside is able to trap the paperhangers. The story was actually more involved but this was Ironside's method of catching the crook.

Little did I know, but while I was away working out the solution, the executive producer had put through a deal obligating the studio to buy the story. I turned in the revised story with the dumpster solution and he called me to tell me he loved it and set a meeting for me to come in and talk about whether I was going to do the script. I called Jim and said, "What do I do now? I've never written a script." Jim told me to go in and tell the executive producer that although I had never written a script, I would do a better job for him than his hacks at the studio because it was more important to me than it was to them and that they were only going to pay me $2,600 and they pissed that much away on a mistake on every show.

Three days later I sat across from the executive producer who was known to many as a tyrant and repeated what Jim had told me to say word for word. There were about five life-threatening seconds of silence and then the executive producer started to laugh. No one had ever talked to him like that. He sent me home to write my first script.

By this time I had rented a small office next to Jim's in the building of an electrical contractor. I sat down to begin my script with Eskimo Jim busy writing in the next office. We had a door between offices. I had bought a new $69 Adler portable typewriter and gotten rid of the Underwood upright that I had bought for $25 (You might ask how someone with my background learned to type? Good question. I believe that God uses our human nature to his advantage. I had taken typing during my short stay in high school because the best looking girls in the school were in the class and not another boy in sight.) Jim had given me a dozen scripts for reference and away I went... for about half a page.

Jim sat in his office trying to write and listening to the silence coming from my office as I looked through every script he had given me. After more than thirty minutes, I threw open the door between our offices and asked, "How do you stop the camera from moving?" I had indicated in the script that I wanted the camera to begin a panning shot and couldn't find in any of the scripts he had given me how to bring it to a stop.

I finished the script and had Carol type up the finished copy. With a lump in my throat and a heart rate of one hundred and twenty I turned it in and waited. One long and agonizing week later I heard back from the studio. The executive producer loved it. He wrote a letter to the executive in charge of staff writers at Universal and said it was one of the best first drafts he had read in a while. The fact that it was the writer's very first draft made it even more special. Not bad for a kid who was a phonetic speller, failed every English class and was thrown out of high school in the tenth grade.

It was 1968, and I had started in television at a good time. The producers and writers had self-confidence. The people on "Ironside" were great to me. They set up a typing stand in one of the producer's offices and let me make all the changes in my script necessitated by budget and production constraints. Then they let me be on the set while the entire episode was being filmed. As much as I could let myself feel things in those days — this was exciting.

When the filming of my first episode was completed, the executive producer said to me, "Go home and come up with some ideas and we'll do another one." I was in shock. I had already heard about how doing more than one script for the same show was great for a writer's career. It meant that they liked his work enough to use him again. I went home knowing I could come up with a dozen great ideas.

Five days later I sat in the executive producer's outer office sipping coffee that Karen had brought me with a head completely void of any ideas. I hadn't been able to think of a single thing. I had even watched other T.V. shows thinking maybe I could steal an idea. No such luck. I was furious with my mind. After all the meaningless chatter I had listened to all those years it wouldn't work when I needed it. Karen's intercom buzzed and it was time for my execution — the end of the writer with one idea.

I sat down in the executive producer's office and after a perfunctory "How are you?" he asked for my ideas. I sat hemming and hawing for about thirty seconds and he said, "Never mind. I've got an idea." He went on to explain how the series had been on the air for two years. It was a hit and now had a responsibility to do some shows with social significance as well as entertainment. He had started to hear how teenagers in one of the best upper-middle-class high schools in the San Fernando Valley were starting to use drugs, and he felt it would be a great idea to do a show about the kids from better homes that were getting high.

There I sat. I was the recovering drug addict, and he was the one who came up with the idea. I told him I thought it was a terrific idea and began to list all the points we could make with the show. After a couple of minutes of uninterrupted information, he stopped me and asked me how I knew so much. I told him the truth.

He thought it was great I had done something about my problem and hoped I wouldn't mind if they hired an outside technical advisor anyway. The tech advisor turned out to be a Los Angeles Police Department narcotics officer with whom I had had a couple of unpleasant encounters in the old days. He and I ignored each other.

The show was so well received that the studio put it on sixteen millimeter film so it could be sent to all of the police departments and civic organizations requesting it.

The kid from the streets not only was putting his own life in order, he was also contributing in a positive manner to the same society he had been at war with. Powerful stuff! My personal train, my life, was roaring down the track with the windows open and the light streaming in. But the light was too bright.

I closed the windows, pulled the shades and put on my sunglasses. I accomplished this by filling me and my car with cigarettes, sugar, coffee, sex, sexual fantasies, T.V., multiple relationships and anything else that would create a twilight zone. My constant feeling was that one day they would find me out and make me go away. They would discover I was flawed, insufficient, and inadequate for the task. Hell, I didn't even know what the task was.

But even in my despair 12 years later (seventeen years of recovery) a part of me knew I was on a train being driven by a kind and loving Engineer — but where the hell was the Conductor? Shouldn't there be an Eskimo/Conductor on board?

I didn't know it but I was about to meet the Conductor.

What made the pain especially unbearable by the time I was seventeen years off of drugs and alcohol was that I was also seven years off of red meat (still ate chicken and fish), six years off the coffee, two years off of caffeine, one year off of cigarettes and three months off of sugar. Sexual or romantic fantasies and television were still biggies but they couldn't hold my feelings prisoner any longer.

I didn't know what these feelings were and had no idea what to do with them. Spending money on others helped a little for short periods of time — until I wound up hating the people I had spent the money on. Also I was spending money on things I didn't need to impress a lot of people I didn't know. Because I didn't know what was wrong I entered a constant state of depression. I just wanted to lay down somewhere and die.

What made the depression worse was I had achieved the kind of income (writing television) that I had always believed would make life wonderful. Instead I still felt insufficient, flawed, inadequate, ashamed, and I had lost the ability to hide those feelings from myself. I had gotten what I had thought would fix it and-it didn't fix it! How could I feel so terrible?

I was in a relationship with a terrific young lady. We brought out the absolute best and the absolute worst in each other. We had been put together by forces that ordained it was time for us to accelerate our healing process or die. We pushed each other's buttons without even trying. Actually, we could push the other person's buttons by just walking into the room. She would scare the hell out of me and I would withdraw. My withdrawal and being emotionally unavailable would make her madder. She would withdraw further and get even madder — and so it went.

This girl had a therapist she was still seeing from when she had gone through inpatient treatment for chemical dependence. She felt I needed to see one right away. Knowing that women were my problem I chose a woman therapist. It never occurred to me that the Conductor would be a woman. But I knew if I got some inside, female-type information, I would finally be able to have a decent relationship and my life would be better if not perfect.

By this time I had been married five times and was in the middle of my fifth divorce. Relationships had been a source of constant frustration for me. I believed with every fiber of my being that if could just find the right woman — the perfect mate — the one who would make me whole, we would live happily ever after and this internal "disease" would go away.

A few months before starting therapy, I had been sitting in a condo with a friend on Christmas Eve watching the "Osmond Family Christmas Show." My then wife (number five) was a flight attendant and away on a trip. The marriage was failing and we both knew it, but not having any communication skills, neither of us said a word.

We were just letting the marriage die a slow, rotting, garbage-type of death. We wore our gas masks at home to stop the smell and eliminate the pain. We left the masks at home when we went out in public so no one would know. In the middle of the "Osmond Family Christmas Show," I turned to my friend with tears in my eyes and said "I'll never be able to have a happy family. There's some god-damn thing wrong with me that I can't stick it out. I can't do it. I'm no good on the long haul." My friend agreed that he probably would never achieve "it" either.

We concluded that we should keep praying and meditating and enjoy the single life which neither of us was enjoying. It had become like cigarette smoking. Some point after having smoked for a while, cigarettes rarely if ever made me feel good. They just kept me from feeling bad when the nicotine level in my body had dropped. Dating had become sort of like that.

In many ways the single life was an addiction, like drugs. The hunt was exhilarating. My best friend said to me once that when we were single and on the hunt, we looked like blind dogs in a meat market, panting, our tongues hanging out, and our heads whipping from side to side.

I was convinced that my life depended on finding the right woman. The sighting would make me forget that I existed at all. Once I had spotted her I would immediately start the screen in my mind — the romantic fantasy — how she was going to make me whole. Then I would put all my energy into the seduction. If she didn't have sex with me right away then I knew she didn't care about me.

There were no long, drawn-out dating situations. There was no "me" so I didn't know how to go about getting to know a "her?' Her willingness to have sex was the indication that she felt strongly about me. (I remember how upset I was when I discovered that women were capable of lust... my god, I could have been used!)

If we hadn't hit the sack by the third date and that was stretching it — I was gone. I knew that she knew there was something wrong with me and I couldn't risk further exposure. At no time in my quest for "her" did I realize that I was searching for me. So there was no way to know that when looking to find myself in another person, I was destined to fail. I was heaping a burden on relationships that they couldn't carry.

You can see why I believed that a woman therapist was critical for me. Of course, the therapist I chose was the perfect one. In my life when I surrender, let go, give up, the right doors open. My decision to get help was a major surrender because I was the person other people were coming to for advice on how to live their lives. My therapist punched my ticket, took my hand, rode a long way (more than seven years) with me before she patted me on the ass and got off to make room for the next Conductor.

Margie Granach, I will be eternally grateful to you. Your Conductor hat is in the mail.

Margie helped me to find my feelings, experience my feelings both old and new and express my feelings. We went back and dug out many of the buried childhood memories. It was a tough process. But then women tell me giving birth is a tough process. Suddenly I lived in my body. I was on board my train.

Conductors come in all shapes and sizes just like Eskimos. I guess you could say that all Conductors are Eskimos.

5

BIRTH LIGHT

*I feel great sadness for those standing in the light who
do not cast a shadow...*

I USED TO BE ONE OF THEM. Once upon a time we came
through the dark, warm passage and emerged into the room
light. We glowed brightly. We were bathed in the light of the
universe and shined God's light on all who looked into our eyes.

Some of us came head first, some feet first, some — me —
butt first, and some were cut out. We made our debut in
hospitals, houses, apartments, cars, trucks, cabs, police cars,
ambulances, cabins, airplanes, even in the wilderness.

Regardless of how or where we emerged — we emerged.
We emerged ready for life on this level. The Creator dropped us
here with a full range of FEELINGS and the ability to express
those feelings.

On the day of our birth we radiated light from the universe,
light from the earth and God's light. The feelings provided us
with the necessary ingredients for a shadow. We were whole.
We were mind, body, spirit, feelings.

I remember when our daughter first started expressing her feelings. I was stunned that this angelic little creature could get so angry. My wife and I, who by this time in our lives, had a combined twenty some odd years of therapy knew that it was critical she be allowed to express her feelings, but I had no idea the depth and volume of an infant's feelings.

I watched as she would double up her fists so tight, she cut off the circulation and her hands turned blue. She yelled with the full force of her little lungs, her face would turn bright red except for the spot right between her eyes. She furrowed her brow so tightly that she had cut off the circulation to her "angel's kiss" and it would turn white. Then, when she was in full swing, she would throw herself over backward onto the floor where she could spread out and really get into it.

As time progressed the only thing that changed was that she would look over her shoulder before throwing herself over backward... a couple of times she had been too close to the wall or on a tile floor. She was learning to express her anger without injuring herself or others.

At three she laughs so hard her whole body shakes, gets so sad her whole being feels it and gets so excited that her whole body trembles. For her the vast majority of life is a joy and all of it is an adventure. I think that's what God had in mind. Being allowed to experience and express our feelings is our connection to ourselves and our God.

When our daughter was born my wife's mother was kind enough to provide us with a nurse to come in and help the first four weeks. Thank God, we needed it. We had read every book we could get our hands on and were still scared to death. Based on our childhoods, not only did we not have any parenting tools – we had defective ones. We were thrilled when Joy showed up and helped us with the basics. My wife was thirty-six when Alexandra was born and I was fifty-two.

Tina had never wanted children, and although I had two grown daughters, I had no reality on being a parent. My ex-wife and her husband had adopted the girls when they were six and three. Prior to that, I was under the influence of drugs and alcohol.

When Tina and I met I was twenty five years off chemicals and had no children born in recovery. Much to our amazement, all we could talk about was having a baby. This was a planned child. We were out in Santa Fe running errands when Tina looked at me and said, "I think it's a good day to go make a baby." We threw away our errand list and went home to do just that.

Both Tina and I are for the most part pretty much in touch with our feelings and that was the most powerful love-making either one of us had ever participated in. The knowledge that we were making love as part of the creation process was so exciting we were absolutely crazy. I am so grateful we weren't drinking, doing drugs, or worried about what would we do for money.

We were not worried about being parents. We had not gone into some meditative state and left our bodies and thereby missed the whole experience. We were present on the train and the ride was one we will never forget.

Joy was terrific. She helped us with all of the basics. She would prepare two or three days' meals for Tina and me. Tina had a C-section and the going was a little slow. Joy was a wondrous Eskimo. We were sorry to see her go.

A year later we ran into her in a supermarket. She knew of my work in the area of family dysfunction and wanted to share a story with us. It seems she was helping another new mother of a three-week-old daughter. This was her second child. There was also a three-year-old boy. The parents had made as sure as they could that the little boy was part of the process.

He had been told and shown pictures about babies and where they come from. He had been allowed to see the ultrasound and listen to the heartbeat. He had been allowed to feel the baby kick. He had been present for the birth. But one afternoon Joy and the mother were sitting in the kitchen having tea when they noticed the little fellow headed for the nursery with a very determined look on his face. Despite all of his involvement, and how hard the parents worked to make sure he still felt just as important after the baby's birth as he did before, the mother and Joy thought they had better follow him and make sure he wasn't going to eliminate the perceived competition.

They watched through a crack in the door while the little boy stood there for almost fifteen minutes waiting for his sister to wake up. Now any of you who have had experiences with a three-year-old know they can barely stand still for three seconds much less fifteen minutes. The moment his baby sister opened her eyes he said, "Tell me about God. I'm almost three and I forgot a lot."

A three-year-old who had been nurtured, whose feelings had been honored, could still remember and didn't want to forget, a moment in time most of us question ever took place... the unification of soul and human.

Our daughter just announced that she is getting too big for her highchair and that we will have to give it away soon. I like her big. I liked her little. I miss her being little.

Without my feelings I have no self. It is this unification of feelings and spirit that is the continuation of the original unification of soul and human. It is our connection with the energy of the universe and our fellow man. My life is meant to be experienced on many levels but my feelings are the launching pad. It is from them, with them, that I am able to get on board the train — and what a train it is.

The track my train travels on is the rhythm of life. The tracks go up steep, steep mountains to wondrous heights.

They plunge into deep dark valleys. The tracks run through forests of mystery and suspense. They sweep around curves of change at speeds that take my breath away. They soar into the sky through clouds of bliss, through the lightning bolts of life past and present, into the spirits of all time. Sometimes the sadness in the valley is almost unbearable but there is no despair. When I wasn't in touch with or able to express my feelings, despair was a Siamese twin to whatever feeling happened to be passing through, including happiness.

So many things that I believed to be true turned out to be false. And every falsehood that was part of my belief system was like an anchor. They weighed me down when I meditated, when I visualized, when I affirmed, when I prayed, when I breathed, when I tried to channel anything but doom.

I believed that there was pain in change. If you were afraid you should do something else... life was a struggle... control of myself and others was the only security... risk was for fools... being spontaneous meant you hadn't planned ahead... I was flawed... tears were weakness... anger would kill me or someone else... if I started to cry I would never stop... the expression of feelings would rip out of me the energy I need for day-to-day living... to be intimate or vulnerable was stupid... affirmations were a waste of time... channeling was for people who had a full supply of bat wings... making noise was wrong... if you didn't need me to take care of you, you would leave me... my solutions had to come from the outside because I was flawed on the inside... appearances are everything... I am half a person... I will be whole as soon as I find the right partner... the list goes on and on and on and on...

I won't take the time to counter every one of these falsehoods, but I will take on a few of them.

There is no pain in change. That's right. There is no pain in change. The pain is in the resistance to change. The pain is when you can't let go of the old to make room for the new. The pain is when fear of the new keeps you frozen on the spot. When the pain of resistance becomes overwhelming and you throw up your arms and say, "Fuck it," you have just surrendered. The pain is gone and you are caught up in the adventure.

I was a very tired forty-three-year-old when I started therapy. I wasn't tired from expressing feelings. I was tired from repressing feelings. I remember one day I walked into Margie's office and announced that I had no time to get into anything heavy that day. We had problems on the television show I was working on and I needed to get straight from therapy to the studio and write a couple of three or four page scenes that would be filmed that afternoon.

Well, as much as Margie loved me, the statement that I had no time to get into anything heavy was like a red flag. During that hour I cried and sobbed and beat the couch. I curled up into a fetal position and tried to ward off the blows of my mother (my newly uncovered memories) and yelled and screamed. When I left Margie's office, I just sort of waddled out the door.

I knew I was finished on the television show. I knew I was going to go into my office at the studio and sit in my chair like a limp dishcloth, lay my head down on my typewriter and sleep. Right? Wrong. I sat down at my desk and wrote more words, better words, faster than I ever had before. My creative exhaustion wasn't from expressing my feelings, it was from trying to keep the feelings hidden from myself and others. My emotional exhaustion wasn't from letting my feelings take wing, it was from caging them.

I always thought expressing feelings was weakness. Strong people looked calm, cool, collected, and confident. Strong people dressed calm, cool, collected, and confident. Strong people kept up appearances at all costs. It's easy to see how I arrived at that belief. In our society, looking good is more important than feeling anything.

I live in a society that spends billions in advertising to support the concept that somehow I will be a whole human being if I just drive the right car, eat the right breakfast cereal, wear the right clothes, carry the right credit cards, go to the right places, use the right tooth-paste, shampoo, deodorant, douche, mini-pad and on and on. If we weren't trying to find our self-esteem-that is, ourselves in our cars, there would be no need for all of the letters and numbers. A car would be a car would be a car. It would be transportation.

But the carnival barkers want you to know that when you are driving a BMW 1745 CSI and you pass a person in a BMW 1745 CS — YOU are the superior person. The downside to that is when the person in a BMW 2856 CSIII rolls by, you know he or she is the superior person.

I have a friend who can afford luxury automobiles and he always has the numbers and letters removed. I have been with him when people have pulled up and asked him the model he was driving. They didn't know how to feel, were they superior or inferior? He doesn't tell them. He only gives them the make, which they already know.

One of the killing results of having received less than the nurturing needed when you were a child is that you spend your life focused outside yourself. Now, there are many people who will praise you for spending your entire life focused on others — but— and for me this is a huge but — when I am giving of myself to others and trying to avoid my feelings, I have the ability to lose myself entirely in the action. If I am not present in my body when I am trying to give emotional support to someone, it can be like giving monopoly money to a homeless person.

I need to be inside myself to receive the power of the universe and pass it on. For me, anything else is either an empty intellectual exercise so I can tell my friends how wonderful I am, or it is one more addiction I use to escape my feelings.

We live in the desert and the first
rain of summer is about to fall. The
scent is intoxicating. I feel alive, part
of, a child of, the universe, blessed.
Funny, I have never seen them
advertise rain. Without feelings I
don't exist.

I remember wanting to be alone rather than in any situation that might make me feel something. Some people try to isolate in the name of God or enlightenment. I know, in certain quarters there is great praise heaped on people who isolate and meditate. I don't agree. I don't believe God put us here to isolate.

If God had wanted us to isolate then the Great Creator would have given each of us our own star. Life is out there moving around with other humans and in here inside of us. The trick is to learn to go deep inside, while also out here participating in the adventure — to be a part of, to contribute to, to draw from, to have FUN. I have known and spent time with people who have devoted much of their life to isolation and

48

meditation, and I never found myself wanting what they had. Now I know people who have met the same folks and said they saw the universe in their eyes. When I looked in their eyes, I felt like filing a missing person's report.

6

WHO ARE THOSE GUYS?

They're the ones that kept blowing out the candles.

GETTING FROM A PLACE OF FROZEN FEELINGS to today has been a real adventure.

During the first or second visit with my therapist she took me on a fantasy walk and introduced me to my inner child. I can't figure out whether to relate the experience here. I went into it in detail in my first book. The reason this is a difficult decision is I can't stand authors who constantly refer to their other book or books. But, I also can't stand authors who consistently put the same information in book after book. It's amazing I ever read anything.

I describe the fantasy walk in I Got Tired of Pretending. (re-published on Amazon 2016) It's a detailed account of my struggle with and healing of family dysfunction. It is written by the guy on the couch instead of one in the chair. The book also contains good basic information on family dysfunction and its cause and effect.

The first meeting with my inner child was to begin eight years of an incredible adventure. Painful? You bet. But trying to avoid the pain was keeping me prisoner. Experiencing the pain was setting me free. My childhood was lost to me. I had only two conscious memories between birth and age fifteen. I had repressed that period of my life and told myself that it wasn't important. I got tremendous support for that concept from people in recovery and the metaphysical movement. They didn't want to experience their pain either.

I met a fascinating cast of characters. No, they weren't in a group. They were all the characters I had created in order to survive. Here are some of them.

There was "**Bob the Spiritual Giant**". He was the one who when my third wife died four months after we were married who barely shed a tear. He walked around being strong and spiritual. He would tell all who would listen (and there were many) how God had taken her home and now he had an angel. Her name was Taylor. She was a remarkable, special woman. I miss her still.

"**Bob the Caretaker**" would drive a hundred miles to take you to the best doctor. He would let his dinner get cold while he talked on the phone with someone and yet would drive himself to the nearest quack and wouldn't interrupt anyone to ask for help even if he were bleeding. By losing myself in others — by letting them decide what kind of day I was going to have — I successfully continued to stay cut off from my feelings.

"**Rescuer Bob**" needed women he could rescue — women whom he could shelter. He worked hard at keeping them dependent. Not much effort went into helping them become the very best person they could be. That would mean giving them wings and he needed them to be shackled. He looked great in his suit of armor on the back of his white charger but his armor was rusting from the inside out. Once I had a little bit of recovery, I started working hard to help the women in my life find their independence. I put a lot of energy into them. Of course, it was energy I should have been putting into my own independence because when they found theirs, they frightened me and I had to drive them away.

"**I Need Your Approval Bob**" had a mask for most occasions and those occasions he didn't have a mask for — he didn't attend. He would spend money so others would like him. He would take ten, twelve, sometimes more people to dinner and pick up the check. He called it spiritual, sharing the wealth God had provided and breaking bread with his brothers and sisters.

I spent tens of thousands of dollars making people like me and keeping the peace. Do I ever regret any of this behavior? You bet! When I finally left Hollywood for New Mexico, I was broke. I had earned over a million dollars as a television writer and thanks to "**I Need Your Approval Bob**" and the incompetent business manager and accountant who handled my money there was nothing left except bankruptcy and tax problems but they were nice guys.

"**Sex Will Fix Anything Bob**" was a confused soul. This guy knew that sex in his mind, with himself, with women was the answer to any feelings that might be trying to get lose. This poor guy knew nothing about making love, tenderness, gentleness, or intimacy. He thought intimate was how deep you penetrated.

All of his repressed anger came out during sex and he and his partners labeled it passion. He could masturbate so many times and with such fury that his penis was sore for days. If there wasn't a woman — and sometimes when there was —

53

there were always porno videos. He could become so absorbed that nothing else existed.

"**I Love You Bob**" knew only about taking hostages, nothing about dating. He needed to be in love and needed a woman's love. Being in love, being obsessed, was as effective as a drug. If the third date came and went without sex, he knew the girl didn't like him and would move on. There was a "her" and a "them" but no "him." He didn't exist without the woman. And when she said, "I love you," he wondered what she wanted. He never said "I love you" unless he wanted something.

Now the guy who made "**I Love You Bob's**" life tough was "**I Know You are Going to Turn on Me Bob**". Once the newness of the sex wore off, he knew the relationship was doomed to failure. He knew she would leave physically or emotionally. Mom had. So as not to be surprised by her departure and to carry out a familiar scenario, he would pull back sexually and become silent, and zone out in front of the television. When this had taken its toll, his partner would leave as he had known she would from the beginning.

There was "**I'm Fine Bob**". He belonged to an organization where it seemed to him that it was essential to be okay. So regardless of what was going on in his life, he would answer "I'm fine, thanks" when asked. And he wanted to hear the same reply from you. Knowing nothing about his feelings, he didn't want to hear yours. Of course, for his own survival, he pretty much surrounded himself with other people who were out of touch with their feelings. Not a lot of light being generated.

"**Addicted Bob**" could take anything meant to be done in moderation and rocket its use into outer space. Once he had burned out on a myriad of illegal addictions, he turned to legal ones — caffeine, cigarettes, sugar, and sex. Burning out on them, he took up exercise. Eventually he tore up a knee running a marathon. It was critical that he do things with such intensity, such compulsion, that he kept occupied, free from feelings. He took (and occasionally still does) everything to the wall. He and "Spiritual Bob" used to hook up a lot. He would run himself into oblivion while praying to God.

"**The Shadow Bob**" was not a radio show. He was left over from sneaking through the house as a child so as not to get killed. As an adult he continued to sneak through most of life's situations so as not to be noticed. When living alone as an adult, he would sneak though his own apartment — still afraid of waking the sleeping monsters.

This cast of characters, coupled with a few I have probably forgotten, saved my life. I'm still here. I survived being raised by an alcoholic father and a child-battering mother, neither of whom were emotionally in their bodies for an hour total. I owe my cast of characters a great debt of gratitude.

Far too many people don't survive their childhood experiences. They drive under the influence of drugs and alcohol and die in car crashes, they die from diseases that rot them from the inside out, they wind up split off from any sense of reality, or they take their own lives.

My "Bob's" saved my life. They kept me cut off from my feelings. AND I survived. The problem is, when I became an adult in recovery, they were still cutting me off from me. I no longer lived with an alcoholic father and child-battering mother. I kept stepping into the light, looking over my shoulder and there was no shadow. It was time to say good-bye. The prospect of life without my cast of characters, without my defenses, was both exciting and frightening.

I learned about grieving when I said goodbye. I lost good friends. I felt the tears, the pain, the sadness, and the tunnel. When I came out the other side, it was like going out into public with no clothes on... but for the first time since I was a child I could feel the life force inside of me. I could feel the light on my face and the wind at my back I didn't have to have something to hang on to. I had begun to move down the track on the human and spiritual levels. What a difference feelings make. I was alive. I looked over my shoulder and a shadow was beginning to form. I opened some of the windows in my railroad car and let in the light and the wind.

7

THE ADVENTURE BEGINS

*Time to set up housekeeping in your
own home and turn on the lights.*

YOU CAN DO THE THINGS SUGGESTED in this book in any order you want. You can do them one at a time. You can do them simultaneously. You may already be doing one or more of the things suggested. For those of you who have spent a great deal of time in enlightenment, some of the exercises may seem overly simple.

This chapter contains the basic tools needed for acknowledging a self and lighting the candle. What I have done is put them in the order I believe works best. In many instances, learning to make three or four of these activities part of your life on a daily basis helps to shorten the struggle. My hope is, eventually, most of what is contained in this book will become part of your life. I know how good it reels to get free from a faulty belief system. Also, being the rather of a young child, I hope that as more people achieve a higher consciousness, there will be a better chance that there will be a planet left for her to live on.

Those of you who have been in recovery for family dysfunction understand the importance of feelings and being present in your body. The material in this and following chapters is designed to help you continue with that process while also moving into realms of universal light.

Once you have gone to all the work to recover from childhood trauma and found a "self," it can be frightening to try and move into the universe, to try and establish a relationship with some kind of power other than yourself. Regaining some of the power taken from us is, for many, the first sense of aliveness we have known since before two years of age. Anything we perceive to be a threat to that power can feel like death is upon us again. That is just one more lie thrown at us by the Trolls that have been protecting us from our feelings.

I want to repeat that all the methods we used to cut us off from our feelings <u>saved our lives</u> when we were children. Only now, as adults, they block us from ourselves and our lives. It is really hard to let go when there is a frightened part of us that thinks if we do so we'll die. Once we have taken the risk of finding the beginnings of a self, the thought that we might venture out into the mysterious metaphysical universe is almost too much to handle. The aspect of all of this that was new for me was that once I had found a self, when I ventured out into the solar system I took me along for the ride. Now, instead of one more way of getting away, it had become an adventure for which I was present.

After the initial encounter with my feelings, there was nothing as frightening as going back to pick up some of the tools that had caused me pain (like affirmations) or had cut me off from myself (like most meditations). But as with so many experiences, there has been nothing as rewarding. It is that self, the "feeling self" that God delivered on the planet, which is most capable of receiving God's message. Returning to God with my new-found self was a continuing source of gentleness and power.

For those of you who have made New Age/Metaphysical tools part of your life but now have a sense that maybe, just maybe, feeling work will help, I have a few suggestions.

Feeling work, family of origin work, core issue work, can be done in different settings. Family of origin work, core issue work, is, simply put, about going back and finding out where in your personal history there were events or information that caused you to cut yourself off from your feelings. It is about discovering those feelings and going about feeling and expressing those feelings today.

You can do this work in any of the twelve-step recovery programs available. You will find you can do the most in Adult Children of Alcoholics, Codependency Anonymous, Sex and Love Addicts Anonymous, Incest Survivors Anonymous, Debtors Anonymous.

You can do some but not as much (based on my experience) in Alcoholics Anonymous, Narcotics Anonymous, Alanon, Nar-Anon (for the non-addicted spouses and family members of alcoholics or addicts). Also, countless family therapists and counselors specialize in dysfunctional family work.

Unfortunately, an abundance of quacks do the same work. Make sure your guides through the feelings have done the work themselves. Don't hesitate to interview potential therapists. Get references from people who you trust. If you don't know a therapist, there are referral systems in most urban areas or go to some twelve-step meetings and find out who the people there are seeing.

Two things I know for sure. One, there is a power, an energy, an intelligence, a force in the world that is greater than I. You may have a name for the power — God, Jesus, Buddha, Mohammed, the list goes on. Or you may not have a name, it doesn't matter. Two, I exist.

I EXIST. Say that out loud (if you're reading this in public and are embarrassed to say it out loud, say it in your head), I EXIST. I EXIST. I AM HERE (state where). I AM REAL.

Let this become part of your morning routine. Open your eyes and acknowledge you exist. Avoid deciding whether you are a good person, a bad person, a success, a failure. *Just acknowledge that you exist.* Avoid being overwhelmed by the day ahead by pulling yourself into the simple awareness that you exist. YOU ARE HERE

The day ahead will take care of itself if we can open up to life. There is life, there is power and I am part of it. Awareness, acknowledgment and acceptance. Awareness of truth is the light. Acknowledgment of truth is the switch. Acceptance of truth is the act of turning the light on for all to see.

A form of meditation that has been of tremendous help to me is called Vipassana. There is a Vipassana center in Southern California and one in Santa Fe, New Mexico, and I am sure others have sprung up. It is a simple meditation. You can do it sitting, standing, reclining, or walking. The purpose is to pull yourself into your body and into the moment. Let's take a little guided tour through Vipassana country.

Once you are in position, acknowledge what country you are in, what state you are in, what town, and where you are in the house, apartment, hotel or wherever.

For example, I am in the United States of America. I am in Tucson, Arizona, in my home, in my office, in the red chair.

Having done that, begin with your feet and draw your attention to where they are and how they feel. Do they feel great, tired, achy, hurt, tingle, no feeling? Just how do they feel? Don't try and change how they feel. Don't try to relax them, just note how they feel.

Once you have established where you are, where your feet are, and how they feel, move on to your ankles. How do your ankles feel? Your calves? Your shin bones? Your knees? Your thighs? Don't try to change how anything feels. Don't try to relax. Just note how it feels.

Your hamstrings (the back. of your legs)? Are you sitting in a chair? Can you feel the pressure of the chair against the backs of your legs?

Your bottom, can you feel the pressure of the chair if you are sitting or the floor if you are lying down? How does it feel?

Your stomach? Empty? Full? Upset? Calm? Growling? Your lower back? Again acknowledge the pressure of the chair (if you feel it). Don't try to change how anything feels. Don't try to relax. Just note how it feels. Your chest? Acknowledge that you are breathing. Don't try to change your breathing, just pay attention to it for a few seconds.

Your shoulder blades? Upper back.?

Your shoulders? Across the top and where they round down into your arms? Your upper arms? Your lower arms? Don't try to change how anything feels. Don't try to relax. Just note how it feels.

Your wrists? Where are they? How do they feel?

This meditation isn't designed to alter anything. It is designed to bring you in touch with yourself.

Your neck?

Your face?

Your jaws? Are they tight, locked up?

Your cheek bones?

Your eyes? Tired? Ache? Sad?

Your forehead?

The top of your head?

Your hair? Can you feel where it attaches to your head? Can you feel the weight of it?

Complete the inventory of your body and how it feels. For this exercise stay out of interpreting what the ache in the lower back (or anywhere else) means. Leave all diagnoses to qualified people for now. Also, don't project what the ache means to the rest of your day, stay out of deciding that you can't go to work or that your day will be terrible or wonderful.

You are only trying to become aware that you exist, your body exists. You are somewhere and how different parts of you feel. That's all. Keep it simple very, very simple. Life only appears to be complex. You may do this meditation anywhere, anytime during the day or night. It will pull you into the moment.

If you're making love with someone and your head is off visiting elsewhere, a quick version of Vipassana will pull you back into your body. Then you can find out whether you really want to be there. (More later about leaving our bodies during sex.) If you want to do the long version of Vipassana, start with your toes and then do each foot, ankle, calf, knee, thigh and so forth separately.

Go back to your morning routine. You announced to yourself and the world that you exist. You have done some version of Vipassana. Now take a paper and a crayon (preferred) or a pencil and draw a picture. This is not an art contest. Stick people are just fine. Draw anything you want but keep it simple. Just a bird, a fire truck, a flower, a tree, a house, the sun, a mountain, whatever you feel like. When you finish, point to the picture and say I DREW THAT... I DREW THAT...I EXIST. Avoid deciding whether it is a good drawing, a bad drawing, a positive drawing, a negative drawing. It is a drawing. YOU did it! YOU exist!

If you're one of those people who are running on such a tight schedule that a broken shoe string will cause you to think about ending your life because it puts you too far behind to catch up — get up a few minutes earlier. That's all you need to do the previous affirmations, meditation and drawing.

Okay, by this point the chances are excellent that you have some sense that you exist.

Now look into a mirror and say, "Hi, Me." That's all. Don't start making a list of your flaws. Skip the "I am perfect in the eyes of God" routine as a means of avoiding performing an inventory of your perceived flaws. Just say, "Hi, Me?' You may have great meditation and positive affirmation techniques, but for the moment, keep it simple. "Hi, Me?'

Many of you may find the first few times you do Vipassana frightening. You might even feel like you're dying. The reason for that is a great many of us fly into our minds to avoid our feelings. We think, worry, plan, scheme, and fantasize rather than feel. Worrying is less frightening to us than our true feelings.

We wake up and the head takes over bombarding us with how the day ahead is too much for us. We didn't get enough sleep, we got too much sleep, the pain in our back is cancer, we're running out of money, how we're going to meet her or him today and what we are going to say and how messy the divorce will be when we leave our current spouse...the list goes on and on and on. The head loves this power.

We gave it power a long time ago and it doesn't want to relinquish it. So if the head keeps trying to pull you back... and you feel scared to death and like you're going to die... keep going.

All that is happening is that you are in the process of taking some of the beginning steps on the path to meeting yourself. It can feel much like a roller coaster ride the first few times you leave your head and pull your consciousness into your body.

At first you may need to bow your head, close your eyes and hang on. You may revert to some of the methods you have used in the past to cut yourself off from your feeling but be patient with yourself. It won't be long before you will be able to scream, throw your hands in the air, and go for it.

As much as possible when doing Vipassana, ignore the terrible predictions your mind will hurl at you. The first may be that you are losing your mind. The mind just doesn't want to give up its position of authority over your life.

Remember, the mind is an excellent servant and terrible master. The mind is just one of the places where we hide, and hiding there is one of the reasons we don't cast a shadow. Becoming a whole person requires risk.

Our home is "U-shaped and we are
Having a fountain built in the
courtyard. This requires a large number
of people.

64

*A general contractor, a
plumber and his helper, an electrician
and his helper, a brick layer. I noticed a
few minutes ago that the plumber was
digging a short, narrow trench in the
concrete base the brick layer poured last
night. It seems the incoming water
spout was right under where one of the
outer rings of the fountain base will go.
There's a lot to be said for ongoing
communication between people, even if
when what you have to tell them may
not be pleasant.*

Now it's time to acknowledge that help is available. Whether you believe this or not, I want you to say out loud

THERE IS A KIND AND LOVING POWER RUNNING THE UNIVERSE.

Repeat this three times. Now your mind may jump in and start to tell you all the reasons why the power isn't kind and loving. Ignore it. For those people who have grown up experiencing their feelings — life is a wonderful adventure.

Yes, there is sadness and hurt in their lives but there is also wonder and joy. Those living in their minds miss the adventure that has been laid out for us here on this plane — this time around. Do I believe in reincarnation? I'm not sure, but I do believe there is a lot more to the party than just what I can see with my eyes.

8

SPEAKING LIGHT

Because I say so it will be true....
Well, maybe.

AFFIRMATIONS, ONE OF THE BACKBONES of metaphysical work, had me constantly in need of a spiritual chiropractor. I read the books, wrote the phrases and said the words, but I was operating from deep in the swamp of low self-esteem. At the core of my being I was ashamed of who I was, and I wasn't able to write and talk fast enough to pull my feet out of the muck of the swamp.

Somewhere I had picked up the belief that I must be a worthy (perfect) human being before God would assist me in any way. Anything short of worthiness (perfection) left me open to punishment, which by my reckoning came in the form of bad luck. In my subconscious, bad luck is what I believed I deserved. I wanted 'good' in my life. I wanted prosperity in my life. I wanted health in my life, but not having received many life-affirming messages when I was a child, I didn't believe I could have any of it. So if there wasn't any bad luck around, I would find a way to create some.

What is interesting to me is that I was sober and clean, I was free from life-threatening addictions, and I was a working television writer (with a tenth-grade education) but I still couldn't see the wonder that had taken place. Oh hell, yes, I talked about it, I shared with others what a miracle I was, but deep down I knew that my luck would turn bad and I would be found out. By "found out" I am saying that others would see me for the insufficient, inadequate, shameful person I believed myself to be. I couldn't let myself feel the warmth or see the light of the universe. I was nestled in the palm of God's hand and couldn't feel it.

Not only couldn't I feel it, when my not-too-sharp agent who was always having financial problems told me it was time to hire a business manager, I hired his. Now people with a modicum of self-esteem in this situation would first have sought a second person's opinion on whether they needed a business manager.

Well, actually, I did get a second opinion. I got it from his business manager who was going to get 5 percent of every dollar I made from that point forward. Second, a person with self-esteem and the ability to listen to his or her intuitive self (essential to the continued success of any affirmation process) would have taken one look at the agent's life and said, "Thank you, but I'll find my own business manager." The voices from the swamp were telling me

I wasn't earning enough money and I wasn't well enough known for one of the really good business managers to be interested in me. And I couldn't risk having one of them tell me that. That would be the same as being "found out." Ten years later I was bankrupt and had tax problems.

We took our daughter to the circus last night. She had gone once before when she was eleven months old. My wife and I spent the first half of the show watching her face and crying. The lion, tigers, clowns and spinning girls high in the air were big hits. We bought her a plastic sword in a sheath. The sword lights up with a flashing light. Now lately there has been a lot of talk about monsters at our house — good monsters, bad monsters, monsters that the dogs scare away and, especially, a green eyed, one eyed one that hangs out around the pool and in the garage area. Last night I pulled in the driveway in front of the garage. We three got out, my daughter with her sword firmly in hand. She walked around to the rear of the car in the dark. She removed her sword from its sheath and turned it on. She held it out in front of her flashing in the dark and said, "Monsters, monsters, come out, come out." My wife had just finished a book. The title is Warrior Woman. I looked from my wife to our daughter standing there in the darkness with her flashing sword, calling to the monsters to come out. Tears ran all the way down into my smile.

Being able to hear and honor your intuitive voice is essential to the continued success of the affirmation process. If you can't let yourself be guided by that voice, eventually the voices from the swamp will take over and imprison you some-where on the path to your dreams.

I knew some great affirmations.
I am the prosperous child of a loving father
whose good pleasure it is to share with me.
I am the loved child of an all powerful father.
My cup runneth over.
I live, breathe, sleep and eat health.
Health is mine. Yes, it is.
I am the living example of the abundance of a·

loving father.
The riches of God's kingdom flow freely
into my life.
Health, wealth, prosperity and happiness are
mine. I deserve them. No one has the power to
keep them from me.
No human power can come between me and
God's good for me.
I am a good person. I have a good heart.
I live my life to the fullest. I see others as loving
guides on my path.
I have the power to change my life.
I affirm light in all the dark corners where fear
hides.
The right woman makes her way into my life as
I speak this.

I've been married seven times. People have made one of two observations. Some say obviously, quite a few "right" women made their way into my life and I screwed it up. Others have said obviously, quite a few "wrong" women have made their way into my life and I failed to see them coming. I would say the truth is somewhere in between. I find that those of us who have low self-esteem either are trying to drag people into our lives before it's time or unwilling to let them out when it's time for them to go.

I also knew some not-so-terrific affirmations like many of the "forever" ones "Peace and love are mine forever." A more truthful one would have been "Feelings are mine today, tomorrow, until I leave this life." Peace and love are not forever for me, and when I try holding that belief and sadness or anger or frustration shows up, I am made to feel as if one more time I have failed.

The "I AM's" in the face of evidence to the contrary didn't work too well for me, either. For example, saying "I am well, I am healthy" while in the sick bed made me feel like a real idiot or that I had failed by being sick in the first place. I believed that if I were a true spiritual giant, I would never get sick. I have yet to meet anyone among any of the great Guru's anywhere in the world who hasn't been dropped by one bug or another.

Do you hear the perfection requirement in the belief that if I were truly spiritual, I would never get sick in the first place?

The fascinating thing about perfection is that it is unattainable, so I have guaranteed that I will always feel less than, a failure, unworthy. I have read affirmation books that demand you write affirmations a certain number of times every day no matter what.

The implied message is that if you miss a day, it is your fault when the money and the perfect mate and perfect health don't show up. Again perfection: "Don't miss a day." Yes, I know, some people call it discipline. I have yet to meet anybody who went to military school who didn't turn out with some sort of serious emotional disorder.

My life does not now or has it ever lent itself to doing anything every day except breathing and processing liquids. So the "don't miss a day" message guarantees failure for me if I buy into it. And I used to buy into it big time.

Ostensibly, the purpose of affirmations is to replace the negative voices in us with more positive ones. The belief is that holding more positive thoughts will draw more positive experiences into our lives. As far as I can tell, the negative voices

71

come from the swamp of low self-esteem and from the messages we did or did not receive as children.

Affirmations arose out of a need people had to feel better, to bring more positive elements into their lives, to ease their pain. The information that is available to us today — that it is impossible to pump out the swamp without diving to the bottom of it — wasn't available then. People were just reaching out of the swamp for a tree branch.

The interesting thing is that with the tree branch, I was able to pull myself part way out of the swamp. Unfortunately, seeing that I was about to escape, the swamp turned to quicksand and yanked me back. Even as recently as a year ago, a part of me was terrified to let go of the belief that I am flawed, undeserving and destined to live a life of failures.

I was working on a film project and I realized that I still didn't really believe that success could be mine. I am married to a terrific woman, father of a great daughter and in good health. To me that could mean only one thing — money was going to be a major problem. Once I came to the realization that I believed that, I rushed out and bought a dozen affirmation tapes. Some were subliminal, some were not. I started listening to them immediately.

Within a week I was sick with stomach cramps, a sinus infection, had trouble sleeping, and aches and pains everywhere. Finally I went to the doctor who said, "Looks like stress to me?' Stress!!!???? How the hell could I be under stress? I was living in a great house, my wife and child were a continuing source of joy and I was working on a lucrative project. No stress there.

On the drive home it dawned on me that I was bombarding myself with positive information and statements. That had to be it. Immediately a voice from the remains of the swamp said, "Stop listening to the tapes." Not on your life. I can 95 percent of the time tell whether the voice comes from the swamp or my higher self. If it's from my higher self, it originates somewhere between the bottom of my stomach and my groin. If it's from the swamp, it originates in my head.

I had to strike a compromise between the voice screaming "If I didn't stop listening to the tapes I was going to die" and the voice saying "More tapes, more tapes, we are cleaning up the water in the swamp?' I cut back on the tapes. I have been known to overdo something on more than one occasion.

That was a year ago and I am still fighting the belief that I am undeserving of real success, real health, real happiness, real prosperity. That message is so deep in me that it is frightening. I'll get it out, I know I will, but the thought of it being gone is frightening on one level.

It has been with me ever since I can remember. I know how to live life believing that I am undeserving. I can't imagine how it feels to live a life believing that I am precious and deserving, that it is my Creator's good pleasure to give me the kingdom. Just imagine walking around feeling blessed: Having joyous expectation instead of dread. It would be like being a small undamaged child at the circus.

One of the problems with succeeding is that many people you have known for years will begin to hate you, to snipe at you. That is not because they are bad people. It's because people operating in the swamp believe in limitation. They think there is only enough out there for one so when you get yours, they think you got theirs and that's the end of hope and fantasies.

They are left with no choice but to hate you, not for getting yours, but for taking theirs. An awareness that our success will make others angry operates in our subconscious. This awareness is a huge impediment when it comes to sticking with and deriving success from our affirmations.

Beginning affirmations can be like playing ping-pong with yourself and having to run from one end of the table to the other to keep the ball in play. On one end you have the person that needs to believe that you are worthy of health, wealth, prosperity and happiness.

This person serves the ball to the other end of the table where the affirmations are. The hope is that by running to the other end of the table and saying the affirmations, you will be able to return a more positive life to yourself. The assumption is that after a couple of exchanges you will be a more worthy person and the good life you are affirming at one end of the table will begin to become a reality at the other end, and that you will be present in your body and able to sustain it.

Some people believe that just by saying affirmations you can make yourself believe that you are worthy. For many that may be true but it hasn't been for me or those I have traveled the path with thus far. If in the core of your being you believe you are unworthy, I don't believe that saying positive phrases over and over, by themselves, will do it.

So if at the end of the table you served the ball from, you don't do the work necessary to clean out the swamp, one day when the ball loaded with affirmations and the good life comes sailing across the net, you will smash it flat with your paddle of flow self-esteem.

Cleaning out the swamp is a matter of getting in touch with your feelings (current and ancient), experiencing those feelings and expressing them in an appropriate manner.

74

Feelings of unworthiness are stored in the body. The belief system of unworthiness is stored in the conscious and subconscious mind. Any and all things that you can do to attack it on all levels pays off. One of the reasons I like subliminal tapes is I believe they attack negative subconscious beliefs.

Regular audiotapes attack the conscious mind. Work with a group or therapist attacks the unconscious feelings so affirmations will work. But you must attack the swamp of unworthy feelings first in conjunction with any and all affirmations.

Another good form of affirmations — in addition to the written and verbalized ones — is creative visualization. Simply put creative visualization is attaching mental pictures to your affirmations. It is seeing what you are saying or desiring. We arrived on this planet tuned into the energy of the universe.

Early on, most of us had to turn off our receiving set for one reason or another. Even though it is the child in us who turned off the set, the child likes seeing pictures and creating pictures. Words alone can frighten a child. If you are affirming success, the child must know what you mean by "success?"

Odds are the child imagines the worst case scenario of being shoved by photographers and ending up on the front page on the National Enquirer with "Sixty Minutes" rolling into the office. Visualizing allows the child to see what you have in mind. It also allows you to focus more clearly on what it is you really want. I began many of my affirmations without having any clear image what it was I really wanted. That can be a real block to plugging into the energy.

The bible on this subject is <u>Creative Visualization</u> by Shakti Gawain. It is a great book. In it she says the three necessary elements for creative visualization to work are the desire to have what you want, the belief you can attain what you desire and the willingness to accept what it is you are seeking. If you are going to take a path affirming yourself and life, it is a good idea to have a reference library.

Throughout I will suggest the books that have helped me and others. Some days I can do something as simple as grab a book off my shelf, read one passage, put it back and have a vastly improved day.

Creative visualization is one of the exercises John Bradshaw suggests in <u>Homecoming</u>, Bantam Books. I'm not sure he calls it creative visualization but that is what it is. It is a fine tool for opening up blocked passages. Another asset to a "let's live life" library is John's book <u>Healing the Shame that Binds You</u>. He has a third book, <u>The Family</u>-but if you saw the PBS series, save your money and buy Stuart Wilde's <u>The Trick To Money is Having Some</u>.

Surrender is another form of affirmation: a complete letting go, a belief in the endless good available in the universe that can be yours, a willingness to turn left when you hit a wall, a willingness to go through the open doors as they appear, even though you have no idea what is on the other side.

I surrendered when I had run out of ideas, I had tried everything I knew how to do, everything was still going badly and I was terrified of the outcome. It was at that point I would let it go. My hope was that my situation − sometimes my life − would just vaporize into the atmosphere. This was always a good time to do affirmations because there was a short period of time where I was open to new ideas. Being open to new ideas is a major part of what affirmations are all about. Often the affirmations break down our resistance to good.

Whenever you do affirmations or creative visualization, it is advisable to work where it is safe — in a room or a spot that is special to you — somewhere free from distractions. In the beginning of your affirmation work, it is absolutely essential to work in a safe place, somewhere you can relax, let go of the tension of everyday life. Find a time when you won't be rushed by pending situations.

It is perfectly okay to tell your family that you need some time out and take it. Actually, it's good for your children (not to mention your mate) to learn that people need to take time to themselves. A great many people who have lost themselves in their partners and their children don't know that personal time is a right— not a privilege. If you are single, it is okay to tell yourself that you need time for yourself. If you are lost in the rush to fill an internal hole with external things, it may have been a longtime since you took time to be with yourself.

Get comfortable and do either the short or long version of Vipassana. Then try to relax. Finally, decide what you want. Can you accept it? Can you maintain focus? It is acceptable even if you answer "some of the time?' In the beginning, "some of the time" will bring results. Affirmations are not for us to lose ourselves in. They are a tool to build the building. They are not the building itself.

Once you have decided what you want, picture it. See it coming true. Feel how it feels to be in the picture. Be careful not to lose your feelings in this process. It's easy to do. Once you have a solid picture of what you desire, claim it for yourself- both in writing and in spoken words: This or God's (the universe's) highest good manifests itself in my life.

If you can't form a picture at this time, simply write or speak what it is you desire. "Prosperity manifests itself in my life" is fine. But it would be helpful if you know what prosperity means to you. If you have no idea other than more money, that can be okay as a beginning, but you might want to take some time and ponder what prosperity or health, wealth, happiness, joy, abundance and so forth mean to you.

Write about it in a journal (more about this later). It is still a ping-pong game: knowing who you are helps you know what things mean to you, and knowing what things mean to you helps you know who you are.

If at all possible practice your affirmations once a day. If you can't always get to your safe spot, it is okay to verbalize your affirmations aloud in the car or on the bus. In this day of self-obsession (which is not self-awareness), no one will notice!

You deserve the best the universe has to offer. This acceptance lies within the acceptance of yourself.

Let it be known that all humans are children of a loving creator. You are precious. You are an important part of the energy chain that gently binds us all. Your feelings are your connection with your human. They are beautiful, they are to be honored. We live and move as humans while our spirit soars to wondrous places we have never before visited.

9

THE TEMPLE

If you don't scream your body will.

"AHHH, MMMMMH, AHHHHHH, OHHHHHHH, right there, that's it, ahhhhhhhh."

This chapter could use a companion videotape. I noticed in a mail order catalog a two-page ad for Playboy massage videos, for couples. I'm willing to bet if you have any body image problems, those videos won't help. Although Tina and I are big believers in the wonderful benefits of massage, we have yet to buy a video teaching couples how to massage each other sensually and otherwise. I'm sure they are probably helpful in many cases.

The problem Tina and I run into is we haven't gotten past the stumbling block of making sure we receive exactly the same amount of time from our partner as we give them. We time the little foot massages we give each other to the second. Now there are some who would say if Tina and I were truly spiritual we could massage the other without being concerned what we would receive in return. Statements like that used to drive me crazy. The statements served to continue confirming that there was something wrong with me.

For whatever reasons, when it comes to massage, both Tina and I are usually unwilling to give more than we get. This does not make us bad people, selfish people, unspiritual people — it just means we are people — and this is what we need and how we handle one area of our lives.

One of the great myths of our society is "to be emotionally healthy means to be not needy."

In much of twelve-step recovery they have a similar myth- "to be recovered is to be not needy."

EMOTIONAL HEALTH IS KNOWING WHAT YOUR NEEDS ARE AND GOING ABOUT GETTING THEM MET.

The worst thing Tina or I could do is to massage on and on without getting equal time. The resentment would build with every stroke. When we have money for massage we make sure both of us are able to get one.

Despite the ticking stop-watch, when there is distance between Tina and me, when we feel disconnected, the carefully timed foot massage still brings us back into the here and now with each other. It is almost impossible to enjoy the massage without being present in our bodies.

I haven't always been an advocate of massage. I had no desire to take my clothes off in front of anybody I wasn't going to have sex with. (If memory serves me, even the first few years of sex partners took place in the dark until I discovered drugs which hid my shame from me.) As I progressed in the process of getting in touch with and expressing my feelings, I became more comfortable in my body.

The unification process of body and self through feelings is a great adventure. The more comfortable I was in my body, the more willing I became to take care of my body. I began to feed it better foods, exercise regularly, sleep the seven or eight hours I require and I took it out to try 'body work'.

At first I was as ill at ease as I had been with every new situation as far back as I could remember. I didn't know how to act, how to lie, how to breathe how to respond, what to say. It never dawned on me that not having had an experience before, I wasn't expected to know anything. I never told the massage therapist I was new to massage.

When they asked if I had had massage before, I said yes. The massage therapist would then ask what I wanted or needed. I didn't know. They told me to tell them if they were working too deep. Right, sure, you bet I was going to tell some hundred pound woman that she was hurting me.

I suffered through some tough massages until I stopped making them endurance contests. Of course it wasn't easy for the therapist. I was basically like a plank on the table. Eventually I started speaking up and telling the therapist I was new to massage. Amazing what I learned.

Some of the types of body work I have had are Shiatsu, Swedish massage, acupressure, Trager, deep tissue, Reflexolgy, Rolfing and a few that were designed for the masseur by his or her spirit guide.

Yesterday I witnessed the dead communicating with the living. After we moved to Tucson we needed to find doctors for my mother-in-law and our daughter. A physician friend of mine recommended a pulmonary doctor for my mother-in-law. We went to see him, liked him and discovered he had built the house we had bought (we purchased it from the second owner).

One day about six weeks ago one of the men doing some work on the house found a clip-on bookmark buried in the yard. It was one of those tie clasp types. It had a female name on it, and for sake of the doctor's anonymity I will say Susan Smith. I figured it must have belonged to one of the doctor's children so I gave it to my mother-in-law and asked her to give it to the doctor next time she saw him.

Six weeks went by and this weekend my mother-in-law started feeling lousy again. This morning we made an appointment for the afternoon. Once in the doctor's office, my mother-in-law handed the doctor an envelope that contained the bookmark, telling him it must be one of his children's.

I had forgotten all about it. He opened it up, took out the book mark and turned pale. I knew something had happened, but we didn't know what. After a moment he explained it didn't belong to one of his children. It belonged to his ex-wife, and she had died the day before.

Back to massage. For a few minutes I am going to get current with body work. I just came back from the chiropractor where I received a minor adjustment to eliminate some pain. The pain was the result of learning how to play golf without making mistakes.

I had never played golf up until two weeks ago. The game had never caught my interest. I had never come across any-one who was enjoying the game. They were either winning or losing a fortune breaking or throwing away their clubs and had no time for other aspects of life.

Since we moved to Tucson I have become acquainted with Chris, a good guy. Chris has a very Zen attitude about golf. He says the illusion is that there is a ball. Listening to him talk about the Zen of golf and primal men gathering together with their clubs to go on a hunt made me curious. He also talked about the beauty of many golf courses and how two hundred years ago this type of manicured lawn and garden was the exclusive domain of the rich.

One day I consented to go to a driving range with Chris and hit golf balls. Ooops! I mean go to a driving range and sweep the grass with the club as there is no ball. I had a great time and was the recipient of some highly supportive praise from Chris and, although I was just sweeping the grass, a little round white object traveled far and straight on a number of occasions.

It felt good to be out. I like male camaraderie. (I used to be a runner but my knees have put a stop to that. I ride my bicycle but not often, so I have missed having an activity that is mine, a place where I go just to be with me while stimulating my body, fueling its rhythms.)

After two more trips to the grass sweeping range, Chris decided it was time for me to experience a golf course. He was telling the truth. It was beautiful. Chris invited along another friend who was just learning the game, and the three of us had a great time. We didn't keep score; we just swept the grass and followed a little white object around. Sometimes the round white object did wondrous things and other times it disappeared in the bottom of a lake. Sometimes it went in the hole, other times it went back and forth past the hole. It was fun.

After another time on the grass sweeping range, Chris decided it was time to enjoy a formal lesson. That was yesterday. John, the person Chris chose to give me lessons, is a young man with a great disposition. But I went to the lesson without being completely aware of the part of me that needs to do things perfectly.

Here I was going for lessons because I didn't know how to do something, and I needed to do perfectly whatever it was I didn't know how to do. Over the years this trait has caused me no end of pain and embarrassment.

Under pressure, I have a tendency to stop breathing. Any of you who have participated in athletic endeavors know that the worst thing you can do when your body is under strain is to hold your breath. Although I was not aware of holding my breath at the time, when I got home I could feel a pain in my back, near my right shoulder blade. I knew it was from sweeping the grass and not breathing.

In the past I would have ignored the pain and gone out the next day to sweep the grass again, just to show I was okay. A lot of that stems from my childhood. My parents made it very clear that being needy wasn't okay and being sick is being needy.

I spent most of my life taking other people to the good doctors, while if I took myself at all it was to the closest doctor. Usually I waited until I had to take myself to an emergency room to get treatment.

Today, I know that I am precious, valuable and deserve the best of care. Last night I called and arranged a massage. If I couldn't get the back fixed, at least I could get all of the muscles around the area relaxed. The therapist did a great job. After the massage I took an anti-inflammatory (I'm a sometimes herbs, homeopathic, holistic, sometimes traditional medicine guy) and slept like a log. I then took myself to the chiropractor this morning.

She said I had pulled out a rib-end and she made the appropriate adjustments. She said I should take a couple of days off from sweeping the grass. No problem. A few years ago pain ceased being a badge of honor and an indication that I'm alive. I finally became too valuable to risk injuring myself to prove to people that I was okay and that I deserved to live.

I remember when I was running I would come up to a large intersection and about fifty yards before I would lengthen my stride, kick my heels up to my butt, pick up my speed and cruise through the intersection trying to look like Alberto Salazar. This little burst of speed and form would usually take so much out of me that I would have to shorten my run by two or three miles — all of this to impress people I didn't know and would probably never see again. I wonder what people with an abundance of self-esteem do with their free time...?

It is now four days later. I took three days off. I went out yesterday and swept the grass again. Today I feel like a hot knife is stuck in my back.

According to John and Chris, my problem is that the ape in me has taken over my swing. I am able to stand flat footed and hit the ball reasonably far with some degree of accuracy, but I have trouble following through, trouble coming up on one toe while balancing my weight on the outside of my other foot. John gave me methods to correct the problem. Chris told me to have a talk with the ape and explain that just because he has a club in his hands doesn't mean that he is in charge.

There is another element here. I have a short right leg. My resistance to coming up on my toe could be that I'm starting in a hole. I am enjoying sweeping the grass but I can't endure this kind of pain. Perhaps if I put a lift in my shoe it will help correct the problem. That means going out to find shoes that will hold my orthotics (a device for correcting the position of my feet) and getting a lift added... damn it's a lot of work to take care of me. I probably should have gotten a lift before now but it hasn't caused me pain. *Interesting philosophy!!!*

My favorite body work is a combination of Shiatsu and Swedish. I find my body responds nicely to the penetration and muscle manipulation. I used to enjoy Trager, which is a gentle rolling, stretching, shaking kind of a massage. The problem was that once I left Los Angeles I couldn't find anyone who did it gently enough for me.

Trager is taught in Hawaii and, ironically, that's where I had my worst experience. According to the therapist, she worked directly with Trager himself. That may be true but being on her table was like being on a medieval torture rack. This was in 1983, and I was in Hawaii to run my first marathon. It was four years after I started therapy, and my self-esteem was much improved, but not so much that I didn't go back to the woman three times, even though right after the first time my knee started giving me trouble when I ran.

In times of muscle trauma, I have found acupressure helpful. Whenever possible I make sure the person doing the work has been recommended to me by someone whose judgment I trust. A big part of making acupressure successful for me has been the ability to breathe into the traumatized muscle to help let it go. Breathing into a muscle is nothing new for women who have experienced childbirth.

But for you fellows out there, you close your eyes, take a deep breath and as you take the breath you envision the air traveling through your body to the desired location. You hold it for a moment and then let the muscle tension out as you exhale. It works. And when someone is helping the muscle let go— it works even better.

Shiatsu is also great. Of all the types of massage I have experienced, it is the one that requires the most commitment. I didn't begin to feel the real effectiveness of Shiatsu until about the tenth week of going once a week. From that point on it was wonderful. I would leave reeling both relaxed and energized.

For the most part I have had the best luck with Japanese practitioners trained in Japan. However, I did encounter two really fine Anglos, one trained in Japan and one trained in California. This, like acupressure, Trager, deep tissue and Rolfing is a method in which you can be hurt if the practitioner doesn't know what he or she is doing.

Reflexology is my least favorite. Perhaps I haven't found anyone who does it right. Perhaps my body just doesn't respond to it. At this writing it has only been painful and unsatisfying. In fairness to the practice, I know people who take good care of themselves who swear by it. Unfortunately we don't live in the same towns and I haven't been able to try the practitioners who work on them.

As far as I can tell, deep tissue work is a combination of Shiatsu and acupressure. My experience is that it isn't the precise science that the other two seem to be. I enjoy it. The people who have worked on me have for the most part been very good, particularly at helping to relax a distressed area. Some deep tissue practitioners are also therapists who use the massage as a means of helping you to let go of painful, sad and angry experiences stored in your body.

Feelings are energy and they must go somewhere. If you hold them in, they don't just fade away. My therapist had been influenced by Wilhelm Reich, and on many occasions I would be all locked down (armored) and unable to cry the tears that were boiling to get out or unable to get the anger out.

My therapist would put her thumbs on a couple of locations on my face, back and legs. The pain was so great I thought if I didn't let the feelings flow, I would die. The part that amazed me was, when I had finished blowing out the feelings, she could push even harder in the same spots and it didn't hurt a bit. I have friends who have had great success working with therapists who combine deep tissue work with their therapy. In some cases, I believe it has shortened the amount of time required to get a good start on cleaning out the internal house. <u>Again, I can't stress enough to get references whenever possible.</u> If you don't know anyone who has been to the practitioner, have the practitioner give you references you can check.

Rolfing. The first two words that come to mind are pain and change. Rolfing brought up feelings in me so deep that I'm not sure even my subconscious knew they were there. Rolfing is designed to unlock those muscles and connecting tissues that have the capacity to turn you into an emotional or physical cripple.

Some sports medicine doctors in Southern California use Rolfing to help athletes overcome injuries. In fact, that was my first encounter with Rolfing. I had gone down to Gold's Gym with a couple of friends to work out. Having never been there before, I wanted to make a good first impression. I put considerably more weight on the bar than I should have and I paid the price.

The Rolfer didn't work on the shoulder I had traumatized. He worked on the opposite one. The pain was severe. The relief was tremendous. I strongly suggest you talk to people who have experienced Rolfing before you take it on. It isn't for everybody... but then nothing is.

If I could afford it I would get body work every day. I am convinced that Bob Hope enjoys such good health because he has his own masseur who travels with him. He gets a massage everyday and has for decades. Most of us cannot afford that. But there are some alternatives, especially if you live where there is a massage school.

We lived in Santa Fe three years back. Students came from all over the world to study at the Santa Fe School of Massage. We discovered that on Fridays they had student massage night and you could get a massage for $10. I remember wondering if the massages were any good.

My wife responded that she would be happy many times to pay someone $10 just to touch her, that her body cried out in need. Money was in short supply at the time, so $10 sounded good. We took advantage of the Friday night special on many occasions. The massages ran from fair to good and were always worth more than we had paid. We have since found that massage schools all over the country have similar deals.

Another alternative is trading. Many massage people I know are interested in doing and learning new things, and they have daily needs like all of us. Usually they don't have an abundance of money and are very willing to trade. You do the maintenance work on their house, for example, and they massage your body. You teach them art and they massage you. You provide care for their child and they massage you. Don't hesitate to ask. You may have a service to offer that you aren't even aware of.

Being in your body and having balance in your life is the main ingredient in living life. Body work is one tool that is indispensable. From a health standpoint it improves circulation, reduces stress and increases flexibility. From a spiritual standpoint it is about taking care of the temple nurturing the vehicle that transports the being. Massage is sensual, nurturing, communication through touch. It is taking time out from doing to just be.

10

LIGHT IN THE VALLEY

Yea though I walk through the valley
there is light.

THIS CHAPTER WAS NOT PART OF THE OUTLINE for this book. On September 5, 1991, my wife's mother died during the writing of this book. The lessons I have learned surrounding this event are worth sharing.

The first lesson is the incredible size of the feelings lurking inside our three-and-a-half-year-old daughter. I had no idea. Sure, I knew she had big feelings, I just didn't know how big.

We've had Tina's mother with us since February 1987. One day in the end of January 1987, Tina, Sasha and I left Santa Fe for Tucson where I was scheduled to do a workshop. We were going to spend the weekend in Tucson and then continue on to California to visit Tina's folks. They had seen the baby only twice. Tina had never really wanted children, and Tina's older sister had died at thirty-six leaving one daughter who has lived in Italy for the last six years.

Tina has an older brother who has a son but there was no relationship between them. So Tina's mom and dad had long since given up hope of anymore grandchildren. Sasha was the apple of their eye. No sooner had we arrived in Tucson than Tina got a call from her mom saying her dad was sick and she didn't know what to do. Up to now it had always been Tina's mom going to the hospital. Tina got the facts. She instructed her mother to get her dad put in the hospital. Then she left for Nipomo, California, where her parents were. I stayed on to do the workshop and planned to fly up and join them on Sunday.

Her parents had just moved to Nipomo. Before that they had a great house in Cambria, California. Cambria is on the ocean, nestled in the pine trees on a hillside. Tina's dad had decided they should move closer to friends in case anything should happen to him. 'Premonition time'.

There was one spare bedroom for Tina and me in the Nipomo house. We let Sasha sleep in the living room in her portable crib. A week after we arrived my mother died. The next day Tina's father died. Five days after he died, my twenty year old stepdaughter by a previous marriage was found dead in an alley in Toronto, Canada, from an overdose. My mother and I weren't close, but the death of my step-daughter ripped at my insides.

Tina's dad had gone into a semi-coma his second day in the hospital and spent his last days moaning, groaning and crying out to people no one could see. His death was a relief for all.

Tina's mother and father had been married for fifty-four years. Tina's mother, who was dying of emphysema, was devastated by the death of her husband. Her bright spot was the presence of her granddaughter. Tina's mom, Didi (pro-nounced deedee) — a name bestowed on her by her granddaughter — had been in and out of the hospital herself over the last two years.

In fact every time we got ready to leave after a visit, she would go into the hospital the night before we were scheduled to depart for home. Tina wanted to have Didi with her for however long she had left. Besides loving her mother, Tina knew she would be constantly on the road between Santa Fe and Nipomo to take care of her. I was okay with the idea of having her mom with us because Sasha loved her Didi and I had never had grandparents. I share my best friend Tom's belief that every child needs "a cookie person?"

However having Didi with us presented some problems. First, because of her emphysema, she couldn't move to the high altitude of Santa Fe.

Second, the house in the Black Lake section of Nipomo wasn't big enough for all of us and Tina and I did not like Black Lake. Black Lake had a committee for everything. You never had to have a direct confrontation with a living human being. If your neighbor's wind chime was too loud, you simply called the brown-shirted noise committee and they would take care of it for you with a letter to the culprit.

For example, we had an extra car we couldn't get in the garage, thereby violating the parking regulations. Forget the fact that Didi's husband had just died. We were breaking the rules and they made sure we knew.

So third, we had to pick a place to move to. Tina was born and raised in Southern California and had no intention of going back. I had lived in Southern and Northern California for forty-one years and had no desire to go back.

Fourth, we had to sell both houses. Tina's mom would be of no help here. She had been nicknamed Dodo (pronounced dough-dough) after the bird by her husband and children. Whether she ever had the ability to take care of business matters we'll never know. She hadn't been given a chance, and by this point in her life, she believed she couldn't. (At first Tina and her mother and father were trying to get Sasha to call her grandmother Dodo. When I heard that I said, "No way is our daughter going to grow up thinking it's okay to call people demeaning nicknames." Sasha came up with the name Didi on her own.)

Fifth, because of Didi's condition she was unable to help with the packing and moving.

Tina and I loved Santa Fe. We loved our little hundred year-old, two-bedroom adobe house. I was living in Santa Fe when we met. Our daughter was conceived in Santa Fe. We were married in Santa Fe. I had written my first book in Santa Fe. We had made friends with people we cared about.

Writing this makes me wonder why we left. We had reasons. One was a large number of people from the entertainment industry and elsewhere who will live only where it's "IN" had started crossing the border. Two, we had a fantasy about living somewhere free from distractions where Tina could paint and I could write — someplace rural, with horses and wide-open spaces. Santa Fe was losing that.

On our many trips from Santa Fe to California we had spent the night in Kingman, Arizona. Kingman is a rural town on Interstate 40. It has wide-open spaces, beautiful mesas, and is only 3,000 feet above sea level. The woman working the desk at the Holiday Inn where we stayed had always been friendly so Kingman seemed like a good idea.

We were in Nipomo five months waiting for the two houses to sell. Tina and I had walked out the door of our home in Santa Fe in January. It was June and we had not set foot back in our home. We had a house-sitter looking after the dog and the cats.

Our house in Santa Fe sold first so we went looking for a house in Kingman. Tina and I were completely nuts from being in Black Lake. We found a great big house, in the hills, with playhouse and sandbox for Sasha, and a pool. Compared to real estate in many parts of the country, it was a real steal. We made an offer. It was accepted.

Trying to close escrow on our house in Santa Fe and the house in Kingman was a nightmare. If it could go wrong, it did. And the house in Black Lake still hadn't sold. Normally, when as many problems came flying out of the universe as were flying around the house deals, I would have sat down with Tina and discussed the possibility that we were headed in the wrong direction, that this wasn't where we were supposed to be. Tina would've agreed.

But Black Lake was such a cold, hostile community that I had gone into survival mode and shut down my feelings. I was in "Go Mode." I had become a person doing instead of a person being. Successfully completing the move had become my reason for being. How successful I was leading this wagon train of women, female dogs, and moving vans through the desert would determine my worth as a human being.

I had completely lost touch with the easy-going, intuitive man who loved his existence in Santa Fe. The man took the time in Santa Fe to enjoy the beauty of the mountains, the sky, the plants, the buildings, the art, the man who in winter kept the cave warm for his pregnant wife and 'child to be' by chopping wood and keeping the wood stove going. (Our home wasn't as primitive as that sounds. We were right in the heart of town and had electric-base-board heating. We just couldn't afford it.)

This was the man who regularly participated in sweat-lodge ceremonies with friends and strangers, said the prayers and sang the songs and felt alive, connected to the power of the universe, the man who for the most part was proud of who he was and okay with what he felt. Because I was more experienced at surviving than I was at being present in my body — living moment to moment and trusting my intuition — I had created a situation in which it would be impossible for me to return to me until the "old lady died?' Didi eventually became the symbol of all my distress. While all this was going on, Sasha was beginning to love her Didi more and more.

In July I returned to Santa Fe to supervise the loading of the moving van, take care of the paperwork, pick up the house-sitter (who was going to live in and help with Sasha in Kingman) and pick up the animals. Tina never set foot in her home in Santa Fe again after we left in January. Early on in Black Lake we would hold each other and cry because we missed our home.

Later we would hold each other and cry because we were leaving our home. But we were shutting down. I was choosing survival over the complications of life. By the time the escrows started seeping ooze, neither Tina nor I was willing to pull back and see what kind of message the universe was trying to send us. We didn't have the capacity for that much spontaneity and risk left. There was the added pressure that Didi also couldn't stand it in Black Lake and couldn't wait to get out.

At my mother's funeral I was to get reacquainted with my two daughters from my first marriage whom I hadn't had contact with in over twenty years. They had been adopted by my ex-wife's new husband. It was coming at us from all sides and we weren't on our home turf.

Taking possession of the house in Kingman went as smoothly as the escrows had been going. The woman selling the house decided she wasn't going to get out at the appointed time.

There we were in Kingman, with me in "go mode," two moving vans sitting in town and she wasn't going to get out. If memory serves me, I gave her until noon to vacate the house. Then in my best metaphysical, connected-to-the-light-and-beauty-of-the-universe frame of mind, I told her if she wasn't out by noon I was going to kill her dogs and have the police drag her from the house. I was going to get those covered wagons settled in Kingman if it killed me and everyone else around me. What a difference life is when one can wait for the doors to open as opposed to having to kick them down.

In twenty months in Kingman I met one kindred spirit. He was a young man in twelve-step recovery who was on the verge of a complete breakdown and couldn't make up his mind between homicide and suicide. I was able to get him into a treatment program at Sierra Tucson, which in my experience is the finest in the country. After five weeks in treatment, he returned to Kingman long enough to pack his belongings and get out of town. I told him I hoped he was the reason I was in Kingman.

Kingman was hard on all of us. The caregiver for Sasha who had come from Santa Fe wound up needing as much care as Sasha. Tina's mom couldn't be left alone, which made it extremely difficult for Tina and me to get away anywhere for any reason. The only activity in town that gave me any relief was hiking.

Tina was painting but I was so locked down I couldn't write. I had committed myself to see it through to the end, which, in my mind, was the death of Didi but she hadn't died. I was in an unpleasant limbo. I had lost the ability to live in the moment, be here and now, draw from the beauty around me and in me. I was lost.

I withdrew further into myself. Tina's anger at her mother was surfacing. Sasha was falling more in love with her Didi. She would tell everyone "this is my Didi."

We got a new Hispanic caregiver for Sasha who was wonderful. She took a lot of the pressure off Tina and me. Didi liked the caregiver which made for some peace in the house. The first six months in Kingman Didi stayed out of the hospital. She was able to take Sasha out to lunch and shop at the local K-Mart. Sasha loved these outings. Then Didi turned left in front of oncoming traffic and was broad-sided. Sasha wasn't with her. Didi wasn't wearing her seat belt and got slammed around pretty good. She was treated and released. We had to put in a new rule: Sasha could go with Didi only if the caregiver drove.

On the days when I felt like being Didi's caregiver she couldn't allow it. She would withdraw into herself and her room. Afraid that she would be a burden for Tina, Didi would fight with her to keep her from helping. We kept trying to reassure het that we would stick it out with her to the end. I don't think she ever really believed it until the end came. People with little self-esteem find it almost impossible to believe anyone could truly care for them.

Yesterday we took Sasha to the doctor
to have some stitches removed -three,
her first -and to have her ears
checked because she had started a nasty
cough. There are two wishing-well type
fountains outside the doctor's. Part of
the deal is, Sasha gets two pennies so she
can make a wish in each fountain. She
threw in each penny and both times
wished for her Didi to come back.

After six months in Kingman, the trips to the hospital began again. In my judgment the medical care in Kingman was poor at best. They kept saying it was pneumonia. They would find an unexplained spot on the lung, or clot in her blood that would appear and disappear. Didi, on the other hand, liked her doctors.

Occasionally, Tina and I would get away to Las Vegas, Nevada, for a day of eating and shopping. Las Vegas had never been one of our favorite towns. It now became Mecca.

With each passing week, a depression settled in on me like a wet blanket. The energy between Tina and her mother was terrible. Tina was feeling not only trapped in Kingman but trapped in a dance of death with her mother. She loved and hated her mother for things that went on when Tina was a child and loved and hated her for things going on in Kingman. Tina's heart would break at the thought of her mother actually dying. She found herself wanting her mother to die one minute and hoping she would never die the next.

The energy around the old homestead was very strange. Tina and I felt we were dying of thirst. Friends of ours would come to visit and we felt like vampires as if we were drinking their blood of life. I know Sasha had to sense it. Children are sensitive to what their parents are feeling. Sasha kept falling more deeply in love with Didi. Occasionally, if Didi and Tina fought, Sasha would get mad at Didi, but she always got over it.

After fourteen months even Didi couldn't stand Kingman anymore so we put the house on the market. It took six months for it to sell. Again we had to figure out where to go. We still faced the altitude problem with Didi. Prescott was out. Flagstaff was out. We didn't want to change states — it cost too much money. We didn't like Phoenix. Friends kept suggesting Tucson.

I think part of our early resistance to Tucson was because the last time we were there our whole lives changed.

Finally, we drove down to look around Tucson. It seemed okay. We called two real estate agents suggested to us by friends. Tina returned a week later and checked out some houses with one agent. She didn't find a house but she found an area she liked.

Heidi Baldwin, the other real estate agent, had never called back. Finally, a bit put out, we called her. She said she had been looking until she found our house and didn't want to bother us. Now she had three she felt matched the specs we had given her.

We all came back down to Tucson. All three houses were great — the third was perfect. We made an offer and Heidi and Tina drove me to the airport. I had to fly somewhere to speak. Tina got back to the hotel where Sasha, a new caregiver who had a gambling problem, coupled with an attitude problem and a cold awaited her.

At the hotel Tina also discovered that I had the car keys with me and the alarm was on. She had no idea what to do. She called the airport — not the airline — the airport -told them her dilemma, and made it clear she didn't know what to do. Tina has no problem letting people know she needs help. Tina and the person at the airport figured out I was on America West Airlines headed for Phoenix. Tina was connected with the America West counter. They called Phoenix. An America West representative met me at the plane in Phoenix, took the keys and ran them to another concourse to get them on a flight back to Tucson that was leaving in five minutes. The hotel let Tina keep the rooms into the evening for no extra charge, and they drove her to the airport in their shuttle and waited for her until she got the keys. Doors were opening. People were helping. We were in the flow.

The escrow on both houses went smooth as silk and we moved into our new home in Tucson on March 1st.

I knew people in Tucson I could go to lunch with and talk recovery, metaphysics, God, nutrition, exercise and love. I was invited to join a private men's recovery support group. I was getting some plasma.

Tina made friends and sold paintings. We found a new part-time caregiver, Lindsay Brown, who is still with us. Sasha adores her. Sasha kept falling more in love with her Didi. Didi kept getting more tired and more tired. She used to be able to get out with the caregiver five or six times a week to go to the market or drugstore or take Sasha to lunch.

Now she might get out twice a week, sometimes a third time for dinner with us. In Kingman she used to watch movies in the living room with us, now she hardly left her room. She required more oxygen. It was getting harder for her. She took a turn for the worse and we took her to the emergency room. The quality of care had greatly improved. One of the doctors she was seeing came from his home to check her over before the emergency room doctor could get to her.

Sasha was falling more in love with her Didi. Didi was talking more about how she missed her husband and was looking forward to joining him.

She left the hospital and had a pretty fair month and a half before she started to decline. Didi had traveled the world with her husband. She had been a dancer in the movies. She had been an active duck hunter and had lived on a ranch in her late sixties.

Smoking had reduced her life to where a fair month was getting out once every week and a half with the caregiver— making half a dozen trips from her room to the kitchen — and

101

spending the rest of her time in bed watching a television she could hardly hear and working crossword puzzles.

A month later she had another flare-up but this time the antibiotics didn't seem to be working. On August 2nd we took her to the doctor's office. They put her straight into the hospital. This time the spots were back, the blood was clotted and these doctors knew what it was — cancer of the lungs and cancer of the liver. She was given six months to live at the outside, but in reality more like six weeks. We brought her home to die in her own bed.

We now had to explain to a three-and-a-half-year-old that her Didi wasn't going to be with her much longer. I had no tools to face this. In my family, no one ever died — they took long, long trips. I have uncles and aunts who have been traveling for fifty years. We headed for the book stores.

We found a great book entitled Beyond the Ridge, by Paul Goble, published by Bradbury Press. It is a story of a Native American grandmother who lies on the floor of a TiPi dying.

She can hear the voices of her children and grandchildren who are gathered around her. Into the mix of voices comes a faint voice from faraway asking her if she can hear her mother calling to her. The voice tells her to climb the mountain.

The grandmother's spirit leaves her body and begins to climb the mountain. She can still hear the concerned voices of her children and the crying of her grandchildren. She wants to go back and tell them not to cry.

Eventually at the top of the mountain, she comes to the land of many TiPis. There she sees her parents and old friends. Flowers bloom, buffalo and elk roam, and the sky is filled with magnificent birds. This is where she will live.

The book continues as the family has what I think of as the traditional ceremony of placing grandmother in a tree in order for her to return to the elements from which she came. It goes on further to talk about death and dying and going to another world.

Sasha loved the book, although it made her a little sad. It was an image of dying that her three-and-a-half-year-old mind seemed to understand.

Didi's last days weren't pretty. Just trying to get the pain medication right was a nightmare. It was hard for Sasha to spend time in Didi's room with her. Occasionally, Sasha would go in Didi's room to watch a Disney movie with ten of her dolls to dress and undress. When she wasn't too out of it, this gave Didi great pleasure. As a little girl, Didi had loved dolls. She had had two daughters and neither one would play with dolls. Now she has a granddaughter who spends hours with her dolls.

There were occasions during those last days I was convinced that Sasha's trips to Didi's room were her way of saying, "You can't leave yet. I still need you." When Didi's husband died, Didi wanted to follow him right away. I'm convinced the only thing that held her here was this little blued-eyed child calling out with her heart for her grandmother to stick around.

As I sit here writing this I feel a real need to say:

"Thank you Didi. You stuck around for two and a half very important years in Sasha's life. I know it took courage on your part, even though Sasha gave you countless laughs, smiles and tears of joy. You were her one and only cookie person, a bed to climb into when things weren't going well, a person to negotiate better choices with her parents, 'her Didi'.

When she would visit you would even shut off your television set, which you had going twenty-four hours a day.

You knew we didn't let her watch commercial television. Thank you Didi.

I know some days your heart broke because you couldn't go join Ferris. I know some days it was really hard and you would've given anything to get out of that decaying body but you stuck it out. Your granddaughter and I will never forget you. Thank you."

Labor Day rolled around and Didi wasn't doing well. We were still trying to get a fix on the morphine. If she had enough to stop the pain she was out of it. If she was "with it," she was in pain. It was easy to see she didn't have long.

Sasha now came into Didi's room with us and put her head on Didi's chest, rubbed Didi's stomach and told her good-bye.

We had two dogs at the time. One, Beanie, was a female German shepherd who had been with Tina for twelve years and with us as a family for five. The other, Suzie, was a thirteen-year-old black Lab who had been Tina's dad's dog. Suzie had spent the two and a half years since the death of her master in Didi's bedroom. She slept there, ate there and never left the room except for necessity. It was as if she knew her role was to keep Didi company.

Beanie was a great dog. She was a watch dog. We went to bed at night feeling safe. Age and bad hips had taken their toll. On Labor Day, she could no longer get up. She went out into the yard that night and laid down for the last time. She couldn't even get up to defecate. It was time to put her down. We wrapped her in a sheet and loaded her in the back of the van. It was nine at night. I then brought Sasha out to say good-bye.

She stood at the back of the van petting Beanie and saying good-bye. Tina's heart was breaking. My heart was breaking. I wasn't sure what was going on in Sasha's heart. Tina started to pull out and Sasha called out for her to stop. Sasha wanted to look in the window one last time at Beanie before she went to "run with the spirit dog pack." The spirit dog pack is a concept Tina came up with and Sasha loves.

I headed back into the house with Sasha in my arms. I could feel the pain in her heart. I could feel the awful pain in my heart. Beanie had been a friend. She had kept us safe, and she was going away. Inside the house Didi had a week at best. Inside myself I began screaming, "I don't want to feel this. I don't want to grieve. I have done enough grieving. I don't want the pain."

Another voice announced that I was in the pain, and if I wanted to know me better, into the pain I must go. God, I didn't want to hear that. I got Sasha to bed, and that night, Tina and I held each other and cried. Belle was gone. Beanie was gone, Tina's dad was gone. Didi would soon be gone. People and things from years past were gone. The pain and the tears created space for more light, and a bigger shadow.

The next day Tina and I arranged for some home health care aides to come give us a hand. We couldn't do it alone anymore. Didi required too much care.

At about five-thirty in the morning the woman on the night shift came to tell us Didi wanted to see us. We walked into Didi's room to find her sitting up, bright-eyed and more coherent than she had been in months. Didi was a member of the Hemlock Society and she announced that this was her last day.

It wasn't long. In an hour or so she slipped into a coma from which she would not return. Tina and I laid on the bed with her and stroked her and held her and rocked her. Sasha came in four different times to say goodbye. Again she did it by putting her head on Didi's chest and patting her stomach. We took Sasha and went out for dinner. We came back and renewed the vigil.

About two in the morning we gave up and went to bed. At five the health care aide came to get us. Didi had died. The paramedics came to confirm death. The sheriff's department came to make sure the doctor was going to sign the death certificate. Finally the mortuary was allowed to take the body. All this was accomplished before Sasha woke up.

In Kingman, the paramedics had to come twice for Didi. The first time Sasha was very upset. She was frightened. She cried. She didn't want to see any-one touch her Didi. She didn't want to see anyone take her Didi. The second time she was six months older, and she was able to understand that they were there to help her Didi. Sasha even came out to see Didi in the ambulance and say good-bye. Despite all that I am glad that Didi made her final exit while Sasha was asleep. I may change my mind someday, but I don't think so.

I would like to acknowledge Didi's Tucson doctor. After the results were in and we knew Didi didn't have long to live, the doctor met with Didi and Tina at the hospital to go over alternatives. He knew that Didi wanted no extraordinary means taken.

Didi made it clear she did not want to treat the cancer. She couldn't see the purpose of holding back the cancer so she could die of emphysema. Tina knew this was the final good-bye. A couple of times in the past Didi had thought she was dying, and she and Tina had said their goodbyes— but this time there was no doubt.

I'm sure a few of you are saying, "Why weren't you holding her in the light? Why were you even acknowledging the disease? Why would you give power to the negative?" There are a couple of reasons. First, in my years of metaphysics, I have never — and I repeat never — witnessed the people around a suffering individual being able to raise him or her to a place higher than the individual's own consciousness would allow.

Didi had wanted to die ever since her husband had died. Her granddaughter was no longer enough to hold her here. The emphysema was making it impossible for her to enjoy her granddaughter. Second, I tried that process on a number of occasions. Once, with my wife of one month who was diagnosed with cancer. I shoved the disease from my mind, I held her in the light, I called in all the power I knew how and she died anyway.

Not only did she die, but while I was busy holding everyone in the light; I was completely out of touch with my feelings. I missed the whole experience and wasn't able to experience it on a feeling level until ten years later on my therapist's couch. People around me at the time loved me. I was a spiritual giant. I had no feelings so I put no stress on their lives. I got terrific support as long as I stayed away from the pain.

In the hospital room with Didi and her doctor, Tina could feel her pain and the tears came. Didi told her not to cry, not to fall apart. The doctor told Tina to go right ahead and cry all she wanted and that it would do Didi good to cry right along with her. Eventually all three of them let the tears flow. Didi's doctor liked her and was sad she was dying.

There was no funeral service. There were no close friends to speak of. Didi's wishes were to be cremated the same as her husband and have their ashes scattered together. Two days after Didi's death, Suzie, our black Labrador had to be put down. Once Didi was gone she fell apart. She lost control of her bowels and her kidneys. She stopped drinking water and couldn't find the doggie door anymore.

Last night the battery went dead on Tina's car just as she pulled into the garage. This morning when leaving for preschool in my car, Sasha wanted to know why she and Tina weren't taking Tina's car. Tina explained that the battery had died but we would get it fixed.

Sasha asked if that meant the car was coming back okay. Tina looked at the hope in her face and realized immediately where Sasha was headed...if the car could be brought back, then her Didi could be brought back. Tina immediately explained the difference. Sasha was very sad her. Didi wasn't coming back, at least not on this level where she could see her.

During the first few days spent with Sasha after Didi's death, we talked of the spirit dog pack and looked at a video of two new dogs we were going to pick up in a few weeks. We had made arrangements for the new dogs before Belle the Doberman was killed. We knew Beanie was getting old and had hoped to get the new dogs before she died.

The dogs, two shepherds, were being obedience trained. Yes, the female is named Belle. Tina and I listed the names of the dogs in the spirit pack for Sasha. We put in every great dog we ever had and some that belonged to friends. Beanie is the leader of the pack. Sasha liked the thought of this spirit dog pack roaming the universe looking out for her.

During the first week, Sasha's face would occasionally cloud up and she would say she missed her Didi. We would acknowledge how sad it is to lose someone. She was privy to her mother's grieving. We would encourage her to talk. She just didn't have much she wanted to say.

By the second week her sadness was more pronounced. She would go into Didi's old room and look for her. We had completely changed the room, including having it painted. Sasha still wanted her Didi to be there.

One night about two-and-a-half weeks after Didi died Tina and I were awakened by a scream coming out of Sasha that sounded like someone had a sizzling branding iron placed against her skin. We ran to her room to find her sitting up in her bed screaming in desperation. It was as if she felt if she could scream loud enough, deeply enough, the pain would go away.

We asked what was wrong. She said, "I'm upset. I want my Didi." She didn't want to be touched or talked to. All Tina and I could do was sit on the floor beside her bed to let her know we were there and that what she was doing was okay.

The screams filled the house. They filled the desert surrounding the house. I hurt for her, my insides cried out for her. But somewhere was a primal recognition of that place inside of her where she had gone. It was as if Sasha was showing me a picture from my earliest childhood, which I knew was me but had no conscious memory of.

The screaming lasted about twelve agonizing minutes. At the end, Sasha was ready to be held. The tears came. She returned to bed with us and slept as if she had been drugged.

The screaming recurred three more times in the next three weeks.

I was stunned that Sasha's feelings were so huge. My therapist had always said that one of children's biggest problems was their size. Because they are small, people tend to diminish their feelings. She said that a horrific denigrating term was "puppy love," and that there was no such thing.

A young person's love is as huge and as consuming as an adult's. I sat in the bathroom one night after Sasha had finished a grieving episode and was tucked in our bed with Tina. I cried tears of joy that I had been able to be part of creating a safe place for our daughter to get to emotionally and express feelings this huge.

For every tear of joy, there was a tear of sadness for myself. Where had my truly giant feelings gone? Having repressed my feelings for so many, many years, almost any feeling seems big today. But watching our daughter showed me I can go deeper.

The power of life: is in those huge hidden feelings. The light and our shadow, our self, waits for us. Feelings were not given to us to avoid, to run from, or to anesthetize. We learned how to do that when we were very young.

Another purpose of this chapter is to show that this book isn't being written in a vacuum. Life and death go on. There is a natural God-given rhythm to life which is:

Most of us spend the majority of our time trying to change it into this:

_____

A straight line on a monitor in Intensive Care would mean we had died. Does it bother you that perhaps the majority of your life has been spent trying to die instead of trying to live? Sure, it's lousy to be at the bottom of the loop where death and dying and illness and apparent setbacks lurk. But if you can't be there at the bottom of the loop, you can't be present when life is at the top of the loop. A verse from the song "The Rose" comes to mind:

It's the heart afraid of breaking that
never learns to dance.

It's the dream afraid of waking that
never takes the chance.
It's the one who won't be taken who
cannot seem to give,
And the soul afraid of dying that never
learns to live.

It is my belief that Sasha will be on the firing line of life. She will be laughing, screaming, crying, yelling, angry, sad, happy, afraid but going forward. And if Tina and I keep about our business, we will be standing there beside her.

Give me the roller coaster of life.
I only seem to get calluses on the
Merry-go-round.
Eventually on the roller coaster I
reach high for the sky.
On the merry-go-round I wind up
hanging on tighter and tighter for
fear of falling off
On the roller coaster I scream.
On the merry-go-round I am quiet
so as not to disturb the sleeping.
Yes, Mr. Carnival Worker, here is my
ticket. Put me in the front car
please and release the brake so
that I may fly to the moon with
my teacher sent to me by God.
Her name is Sasha.
She lives in the land of light
and casts a huge shadow.

11

JOURNALS

*How do I know I am telling myself
the truth?*

JOURNALING IS ONE OF THE "GETTING TO KNOW yourself exercises" with which I have run hot and cold. I go for a period of time never missing a day in my journal and then miss a couple of years. I have friends who have journaled faithfully for years. It is as much a part of their daily life as breathing.

Despite my on-again, off-again behavior with journaling, I am a firm believer in its benefits. In the beginning it seemed I journaled only when I had problems in my life that were crushing my chest. I would write like crazy, trying to figure out a solution.

The sample below from 1967 is representative of how I would look for what to say, for whom to say it to, and for when to say it — all in order to change my life. I didn't yet understand the function of journaling was to get to know myself

[A vote has been taken by those that make editorial decisions and it has been decided that I am the only one who can read my writing. Instead of making copies of the actual pages I will transcribe them. I have an opportunity here to make myself look very wise. Fortunately or unfortunately, depending on how you look at it, I know the value of self-disclosure.]

May 7, 1967

I could be assistant foreman at this goddamn
sweat shop if Glen wasn't afraid I am smarter than
he is. The trick here is to act stupid and start eating
lunch with him and his cronies and talk about
boats and fish and campers and all the rest of that
crap. I hate it that I don't make more money.
Maybe the move here is to start spending more
time with the engineers. Naw that'd piss Glen off.
Lunch with the boys is it.

I wanted a raise. Glen was the enemy. I hated talking about weekends in the great outdoors but was willing to rather than continue to be myself. How do I maneuver people to get what I want? The thought of changing jobs never entered my mind because on a deeper level I knew I was flawed and wouldn't get such a good job. The raise was the only answer for my life situation. The raise would mean I could buy a car, she would love me, life: would be beautiful.

Needless to say twenty-four years later I have a lot of insight into what was going on with me then. But at the time I believed that all my problems — and solutions — were external. I had no idea that I contributed to my problems. I always believed if I could just find the right job, the right woman, the right place to live, the right friends, everything would be all right. But now I know I have to be clear on who I am before I can know what is good for me.

Occasionally, I would come close to what I perceived to be perfect surroundings — but then either they or circumstances — would do the horrible, unforgivable act of changing. Believing my good is somewhere external to me is a very limiting belief. There is only one right job, one right amount of money, one right woman... so when others hit it big... I thought they had received mine and my dreams were shattered.

Fortunately, I was surrounded by people with about as much self-esteem as I had. They would make a momentary connection with the energy of the universe and good would flow into their lives. They would just as suddenly screw it up and it would disappear.

One of the functions of journaling in my life is to show me how in years gone by I have handled change. This was valuable information when I was doing my family of origin work and needed to find out when I was surviving as opposed to living, where I was locked down, when my absence of self-self-esteem — created so much fear of exposure that I couldn't go with indicated changes.

Seeing how I had handled these situations helped me start to trace my feelings backwards. I found out what had happened to set me up to be so afraid of being present and taking chances in my own life. I got to where I could encourage you to take chances even though I felt like I was being left behind. Once I understood the cause of a lot of my behavior it became, not only possible but, easier to change. What a relief! I don't mind feeling out of control when it is the universe running the show. But when it's my history, when it's a past that I can't remember, that is running the show, it's very frightening.

One of the things I learned going over old journals was that being in survival mode reduced the pain. When my life was being run by my history, which I couldn't even remember, I didn't know I had choices other than the ones I was making. Operating on that basis made it easy to blame everyone and everything external to me for my problems.

Once I began therapy and began to see the marionette strings reaching from the hands of my parents into my life at the time, my pain increased. I was beginning to see I had choices but didn't know how to make them. I didn't even really have the tools for making them. I was out of touch with my anger, and without anger, I couldn't set boundaries. And watching people stomp through my life was beginning to hurt like hell.

The pages below from a 1980 journal are a good example.

June, 1980

I spend my life at this goddamn studio, should be out having fun. If didn't spend so much time listening to Angie's [my secretary] problems I'd get more work done during the day. She's a single mom with a lot of courage and if I don't care who will. If I don't get this script done I won't be here to care either. I got to stop running to the set with the changes. Send one of the other writers! I'd have more time if Linda didn't always have a ready prepared agenda when I got home.

Angie was a single mom who worked hard. She would also tell her troubles to anyone who would listen. She would go over and over the same material. She clutched her troubles to her breast. Now I try and make myself sound like a good guy because I took the time to listen to her, but in truth I would only listen to her on studio time, not on my time. I didn't listen because I wanted to, I listened because she had me captive and I didn't know the first thing about setting boundaries.

My parents stomped through my life when I was a child and I thought that's how it was done. My having to take pages to the set was another example of not setting boundaries, coupled with low self-esteem.

My office was right next to the producer. He would walk in, toss pages on my desk and say, "See these get to the set." He stopped in my office because it was convenient. He didn't care how I got the pages to the set. I could've sent my secretary. I could've sent one of the other writers. I went because I was afraid if I didn't do it myself they would get rid of me.

At home the same thing, no boundaries. I didn't know how to tell Linda I was tired and needed time to rest. or I had things I wanted to do.

It was impossible for me to make positive changes until I was aware that changes needed to be made. In that awareness was tremendous pain. It is one of my least favorite dynamics of finding the true self awareness... pain... knowledge change is needed... resistance to the change... heightened pain... surrender/willingness to change... relief... change... increased self-esteem....

Hundreds of thousands of people are unhappy with their lives. It is a secret they keep from themselves and usually from their friends. I include their friends because based on my experience, no one living a life of denial, wants to surround him or herself with people who are pointing out the very things he or she is trying to keep secret.

Mary Jackson in Santa Fe, New Mexico, developed a spontaneous self-awareness exercise that I sometimes use in workshops. Basically, it is giving people three minutes to list ten things they enjoy doing. I have conducted this exercise with over four thousand people.

Fifty percent do not list activities that include their significant other. Ninety percent do not list making love. Now anyone who had been sexually abused as a child would not list making love. It wouldn't enter their mind, unless of course they were a practicing sex-addict and that particular addiction was still working for them. Ninety percent do not list what they do for a living.

Having spent time talking with people after the exercise, I found many to be afflicted with the same unhappiness I had experienced. In the final analysis, both people in recovery and people standing in the light just weren't happy. I'm probably repeating myself, but it is so important to understand life isn't about cutting ourselves off from our feelings in order to be able can tolerate what is going on. It is about being in touch with our feelings so we can experience what is going on. Then we will have the power to make choices about our life.

I can hear some of you saying, "I don't make choices, I am guided by the force of the universe, or higher power, or spirit guide?' If you came from a truly nurturing environment, I would believe you. If you came from a less than nurturing environment, I would question your statement unless you have been steeped in recovery from dysfunction for several years.

For those of us who had to cut ourselves off from our feelings to survive our childhood, our survival instincts are so powerful, it is quite easy to misinterpret them as the voice of God. We simply make the choices — using God as a scapegoat — which will put us into situations containing familiar pain, and the kind of situations in which we don't have to change.

This is one of the places where journaling comes in handy. If you are being as honest as you can with yourself, you will begin to see a pattern in the choices you make. They won't really be full of risk or spontaneity. Be careful that you don't fool yourself into thinking that because you moved from one town to another and you are on the roller coaster and not a merry-go-round.

I have moved from one area to another only to surround myself with the very same type of people I just left. Within a short time I was having the same relationship problems I had before I left the last place. Once we find ways to protect ourselves from our feelings, we become very devious — not only with others — but with ourselves.

If you can let yourself be honest, you can start to discover who you really are and what you really want. To write down information from the darkest comers, you may need to make sure your journal is safe, and that no one can find it and read it. A great many of us have a terrible time with trust. Knowing this we often leave ourselves open when we shouldn't.

One of the most common excuses for not journaling is, "When I go to bed, I'm too tired to write." Somehow, somewhere, I and a great many others got the idea that journaling must be done in the dead of night.

Perhaps the early journaling advocates had families with small children and night was the only time of peace they could find. Or perhaps they were journaling on the events — physical, emotional, spiritual — of the day, and began their writing when the day was complete.

No matter what the reason, night is not the only time one can journal. The best time to journal is the time that works best for you. Journal when you are most vulnerable and around the time when you come closest to telling yourself the truth.

Nowadays, the most common time for me to journal is on airplanes. I have no idea why. Maybe I figure if the plane goes down, I'll be dead and won't care who reads it.

This morning Sasha was lying in bed
with us and leaned over to talk to Belle.
She petted Belle and Belle licked her.
Sasha called her a honey and a dear
and told her that she, Belle, was never
going to die.

If you kept diaries when you were young, you were keeping a journal. If you are lucky enough to still have those diaries, they can be very valuable in discovering who you are, why you are and what happened to make you that way. But be cautious. Some people kept diaries portraying their lives as they wished they were instead of how they actually were. These folks usually make dedicated affirmation writers.

I never kept a diary. Early on my survival instincts said, "Don't give these people any more information than you absolutely need to."

Journaling can also be used as a means of tapping into your creativity. An excellent book, The Creative Journal; The Art of Finding Yourself by Lucia Cappacchione shows you how to include drawing in your journaling.

Drawing can be fun as well as informative. The best book for me is one that has a blank page on each side. Sometimes I will do a drawing that represents what is going on in my life, and then write about the drawing.

Other times I will write about what is going on, and then do one or two drawings — a drawing that represents the writing or a drawing that represents the solution.

Other times I draw my dream of the night before, then write about it. I don't use dreams as much as I hope to. I remember only a few.

At the moment I'm not taking the time to make a concentrated effort to do more. On a recent trip to Europe, I made myself turn on the light and write down what I had dreamed. As soon as I get past the fear of losing sleep, I'll do more of that. If I am looking to be a little more creative, I will draw with my left (opposite) hand in an attempt to slow down the left brain.

Much like creative visualization, you can use journaling to write and draw your hopes and dreams. For a short period of time, I used drawing to help my visualization. I am not a great artist — more like kindergarten art — with a large number of stick people — but having the drawing to refer to, helped me concentrate on the image.

Absolutely nothing to do with journaling is about perfect drawings, perfect handwriting, and perfect words. It is about you putting the real you down on paper. I highly recommend The Creative Journal and A Workshop In Journaling.

My best friend, Tom Alibrandi, used to teach a course in journal keeping and how it can be used to write a novel. The idea of the course was to write down everything you could about a current feeling-say for example: anger. Then give the feeling to a fictionalized character. Then give it to a second character. I remember Neil Simon saying, "When writing an argument between two characters, make sure both of them are right." This exercise is a great way to get into the habit of doing just that.

A second exercise Tom used was to kill off the editor in your head and just pour words onto paper. Don't concern yourself with whether they make sense. Just let fly. You might want to use the opposite hand for this — as awkward as it may seem.

Another terrific opposite-hand exercise is to write a letter from you to your inner child. I first saw this exercise done by Wayne Kritsberg. I don't know if it originated with him, but I like to give people credit for tools they have passed on to me and others.

If you have no concept of an "inner child," a number of good books have been written on the subject. Homecoming by John Bradshaw is one of them.

One theory maintains that the pain many of us experienced as children was so great that our child went into hiding. As an adult, that child still lives tucked into his or her bomb shelter, waiting for the all clear.

I support the theory. It was my experience. I go into detail on meeting my inner child in my first book, I Got Tired of Pretending.

Let yourself accept the existence of an inner child. Now, if possible, get two photographs of yourself-one from when you were a small child, age two to five. The second photo needs to be current — a driver's license photo is fine. Next, find a writing tablet, preferably a large one, a pen or pencil and a box of crayons.

The first letter is to be written from you, the adult today, to the child. There are probably some things you would like to say to this child. I had a lot to say about the places I had gone and the things that had happened while I was drinking and using drugs. I also had a lot to say about constantly surrounding my inner child with emotionally unavailable people.

Don't make the letter too long. Children don't have a long attention span. A good way to control the length is to limit the time you spend on the letter to eight minutes. If you can end your letter with a question it will help the exercise. Something as simple as, "How are you? Where have you been?" will work.

Next, take a couple of deep, deep breaths and blow them out. Now, using your opposite hand, let the child pick a color crayon he or she likes. Now, let the child respond to your letter. Yes, it's awkward, the printing or writing is child-like but do it anyway. You may find that you will be more comfortable letting the child lie on the floor, and here too, it is a good idea to give yourself eight minutes to avoid getting too long.

A great many people — myself included — ran into a very angry, distrustful child the first few times around. It's to be expected. If we have continued to cut ourselves off from ourselves — whether by means of a metaphysical tool kit or addictions — the child is going to be angry.

Depending on how you handle your extreme feelings you might want to find a friend with whom to do the exercise. By this I mean, if you are easily overwhelmed by your feelings, have someone else around. Or you may want to check with a therapist before doing the exercise. Some therapists use this exercise in their treatment plan.

Once you have finished the letter from your inner child, take a minute to study the current photo of yourself. If you get easily lost in space you may want to look from the photo to a reflection of yourself in a mirror until you are back in the adult.

Once you have written a couple of letters and established communication with your inner child, you can have some with this exercise. You can write to ask the child what he or she would like to do and let the child respond. Be prepared to go to some strange places and do some strange things.

I used to carry a journal around with me, but I stopped when I found other people couldn't stop themselves from reading it. I believe that our secrets keep us prisoners, but I will choose whom I tell them to and when. For me, it is necessary that only one other person knows some secrets. That person could be a therapist who is sworn to secrecy. In my case, it's my best friend. He knows it all.

One of the early problems I had with journaling came from not feeling safe. I was shocked to find a live-in girlfriend had read parts of my journal and told others. Of course, I started writing two journals — one for me and one for them. What follows are two pages written on the same day. One was in my private journal — the other I left around hoping my partner would read it.

October, 1977 [private]

*I had lunch with Judy today. She makes me
smile. I don't feel so pressured to be a certain way,
say certain things. Why can't Ann get off my ass
at home? I go through the door and I feel like a
performer walking into center ring and I hate it.
Then why don't you leave? She'll get really pissed
If I say I want out. I'll see if Judy wants to meet
me for breakfast Friday.*
***

October, 1977 [for my partner]
*I have spent my life dreaming of this kind of
happiness knowing it would never be mine. I
thought to love someone like Ann was matinee
time — not real. Now I know why some guys walk
around looking like the canary that got away from
the cat. I wish I was better able to express how I
feel. I seem to be quiet too much of the time.
Tomorrow I will tell her how much I love her.*

There I was in a relationship in which the magic had worn off. I was out of dance routines to entertain my partner and so afraid of a woman's anger (from being beaten by my mother as a child) that I couldn't say anything. Someone new, (Judy) was on the scene. She hadn't seen my dance routines.

It was easy to be with her. I didn't have any tools and didn't know what was going on — just that Ann was the wrong girl and every indication was that Judy was right girl. This was a pattern that had gone on for years and was about to go on for a few more. Afraid to tell Ann I wanted out, I followed my father's pattern and retreated into silence.

I already knew on a subconscious level that if you withhold sex and conversation, most of the time your partner will eventually leave. It took my mother twelve years to get the message.

My journaling was showing me there was a problem but I didn't understand the scope of it. The one new piece of information I had learned was that I was afraid of my partner's anger. I had not admitted that to myself before this. I didn't know what to do with the information so I ignored it.

Arm found the various pages I wanted her to read in order to keep the peace and it did, until no matter what was written on the paper my silence and the absence of physical affection drove her out.

If you are not okay with your feelings and who you are, a great way to bring real grief into your life is to sneak around reading your partner's journal. If you are okay with your feelings and who you are, you still shouldn't sneak around reading your partner's journal. Actually, you probably won't.

If you find yourself drawn to your partner's journal like a junkie to heroin, there may be some more self-discovery you need to do.

Just because someone thinks something and takes the time to record it, doesn't mean he or she is going to do it.

I would heartily suggest that everyone looking to move his or her life forward try journaling. It can't hurt. We have added six blank pages so you can practice.

Here are some sample questions you can ask yourself and then answer with words and drawings.

1) What would I change about my life?
2) If I had two weeks to live, what would I do?
3) Why aren't I doing it now?
4) How do I feel/think about my life?
5) What do I think of myself?
6) Did any events from my childhood affect my life this past week? What were they?
7) What would I like to manifest into my life?

This is about getting to know yourself. Be patient. If you haven't done journaling before, it takes time for most people to get comfortable with the process. Once you begin to make discoveries, you can act on the information.

It would have done me a world of good had I been able to tell Ann what was going on as far as I understood it. Yes, we probably would have fought — but for me that would have been progress. It would have been much more desirable than my sneaking around.

JOURNAL

Journal

.

Journal

Journal

Journal

Journal

Journal

Journal

Journal

Journal

Journal

12

GARBAGE IN-GARBAGE OUT

*Taking the time to take care of this
temple God has provided is one of the
most powerful prayers I can offer to the
universe. It is the most powerful
affirmation I can utter. To my guides,
my God, myself, I present the beauty
of a moving shadow in the light...*

THE CARE AND FEEDING OF THE HUMAN has been a war
zone for me. Once off heavy drugs and alcohol I used sugar,
cigarettes, caffeine, grease, salt, fat and god knows what else to
continue the process of keeping me cut off from my feelings.

One by one I began eliminating what I considered lesser
addictions. With each one that went away, more feelings began
to ricochet inside me. The more feelings that ricocheted, the
heavier I would rely on whatever addictions were left. This was
not fun.

I have met people who soar through the galaxy with their
spirit, channel other spirits, predict the future and toss the

bones, all the while attempting to bury their human being under tons of food.

I am convinced no matter how much light you bring into your own personal universe, if you are cut off from the human, you will cast no shadow, and without a shadow you are incomplete. It's an incompleteness that based on my experience cannot be glued together in the world of the spirit or filled with food.

Saying it's so — doesn't make it so. My participation has always been required. I can say I'm thin for twenty years but if I don't go about getting information on nutritious eating and exercise, the best I can hope for is losing a few pounds in the beginning followed by gaining back even more because of the depression that sets in over my failure to talk my way into a perfect body.

One of the reasons this has always been a difficult area for me is that it is infinitely more important to my survival to 'look good' than to 'do good'. The simple act of getting some information and some help with good nutrition was not enough. I needed to look great doing it, which meant secrets, lies, isolation and guaranteed failure.

One of the things that helped was finally being able to accept that there was no way in hell I could be any different than I was, based on the life experiences I had lived. I could do nothing to change what had happened to me or what I had done in response to what had happened to me. I was the end result of a process that had begun when I was born.

My shelf-full of addictions was my library for coping. They apparently weren't going to go away in a flash of light. I had tried that one and had seen others try. Declare freedom from all addictions and then lock down, clench the jaw, stiffen up, hang on and try and make it true.

Rigidity and control don't work. If they did, Jimmy Swaggart wouldn't have been picked up a few weeks ago by the police while driving down the wrong side of the street with some pornographic magazines and a hooker in the car. Of all the people on the planet, I believe this is one guy who didn't want that to happen. I feel safe in venturing forth the five-cent diagnosis that he is a sex addict. This is the area in which he can cut himself off from his feelings, wreak havoc in his life, and keep alive the tension that must have existed when he was a child.

The tragedy here is that he appears to have himself locked into a belief system that won't allow him to get help. Jesus has to win this battle with the devil in front of a live audience. It's sad. There are some excellent places he could go to and get started on the road to recovery, but it wouldn't be in a flash of light, the babbling of tongues, or the laying on of hands. He wouldn't be able to look good doing it. He wouldn't be the star. He would be just one more mere mortal struggling with his history. It would be a slow, day-by-day process with temptation lurking in every doorway and probably a couple of new addictions popping up to pick up where sex left off.

My prayers are with you, Jimmy. I'd love to see you in Sierra Tucson or an equivalent facility getting help.

For those of you in twelve-step recovery, can you imagine what a convention speaker Jimmy Swaggart would be? He would have us swimming in tears of sadness and joy. This is a "made for you" new audience for you, Jimmy. No money to be made, but you never did seem as interested in the dough as many of the other hustlers are.

If you are locked into rigid fundamentalist beliefs — although I doubt you are — if you are reading this book — but if you are, is it so hard to accept that all the work being done today to help people heal their childhood and move into the light may be based on information provided by Jesus or God or Buddha or whomever? Is it so hard to accept all of this is a gift to help the children move forward?

Once I was able to say to myself and others "I need some help here with this because this seems to be as good as I can do with the information I've got," I became an active participant in bringing the light into my life. **And this partnership, me with me and me with the universe, is terrific.** I am not describing perfection here. I am describing a process. Three steps forward, one step back — a human attempting to change his or her life with a new library filled with new information.

I have found it difficult if not impossible to stick to a rigid regimen pertaining to food or exercise over a long period of time. Sometimes my eating was good and my exercise was lacking. Then my exercise was terrific and my eating was sloppy. And then suddenly there were shorter periods where both exercise and eating were moving along nicely.

Why, you ask, didn't I just adopt a workable routine with both and go on down the road? This is good question. It seems that life — with its myriad of distractions — constantly throws me off course. The exception is when I am so compulsive and obsessive with exercise as an example — that I allow nothing to throw me off until I begin to chip, crack and get emotional stress fractures from being so rigid.

The first five years of my recovery from drugs and alcohol, I didn't take any mind-altering medication, even if the doctor insisted. Today, when I am trying to heal something with traditional medicine, I will take what's prescribed. (One exception was the time I was under such stress with affirmations that the doctor thought a good tranquilizer would help.

I personally would rather find other solutions — yoga, exercise, diet, meditation — to stress.) I haven't had a drink of alcohol in twenty-nine years. In the early years of sobriety, I wouldn't even eat food cooked in alcohol. Now, if something is prepared in alcohol (as long as it's cooked) I have no problem enjoying it.

I have not had a cigarette since I stopped smoking in 1978. I doubt that I will ever find a need to puff on a cigarette. But if I were confronted with a ceremonial pipe, I very well might partake of the ceremony. When I first gave up sugar, I wouldn't go near any type of sugar or sweetener — the exception was natural sugar in fresh fruit.

Now it's twelve or thirteen years later and I will occasionally enjoy a dessert made with honey. Tina makes a tofu pumpkin pie, sweetened with fructose. This is a spiritual experience. I will occasionally drop in on the local Honey Hill Farms frozen yogurt store and enjoy a honey or fructose sweetened, non-dairy desert and once in a while, a dairy one.

Our daughter doesn't eat sugar and I will occasionally join her for a couple of sorbitol-sweetened Gummy Bears. The exception for Sasha is if there is a party and all the other kids are eating cake, we will let her have a small piece. Usually she isn't that crazy about it, and she is happy to go back to her almost sugar-free existence.

I gave up dairy because I was tired of sinus headaches. My yoga teacher said if I gave up dairy it would be the end of my headaches, so I gave it up completely. That was hard. Dairy was a staple in my diet. I could take three of four bricks of cheese, a box of Triscuits and a couple leaves of lettuce and make a meal. But she was right — no more sinus headaches. Today, there is a sprinkling of dairy throughout my eating — occasionally yogurt with fruit for breakfast and cheese on pizza, pasta, salad.

A terrific cookbook if you are trying to clean up your act but don't want to give up desserts is Honey & Spice by Lorena Laforest Bass, published by Coriander Press.

As a rule, once I have cleaned my system out of a particular substance, I will continue the absolute abstinence a little while longer, and then flexibility serves me best. I find flexibility hard. I want to be perfect and never eat anything that contains any toxic substances as long as I live, never eat anything I've given up and exercise willingly on a superman schedule.

When I moved to Tucson I was asked to become part of a men's recovery group. We meet on Monday nights at someone's house. The beverage usually served is diet colas. I used diet colas as a source of caffeine for about four years after I gave up coffee. Some days I could consume eighteen cans. I thought Rice Krispies and Tab were compatible tastes. About seven years ago, I finally gave up diet colas. While living in Kingman, Arizona, I would occasionally have a diet cola, usually when Tina and I went off to Las Vegas to shop.

So I was going along okay until we moved here. Now, having a ritual beverage with the guys appealed to me, so I began having one or two caffeine-free diet colas at the meeting. Soon I was having a couple during the week at home. Not long after, I was having a couple of six-packs or more at home. I drink colas out of the can, which creates a lot of gas. I hate the bloated feeling — and I love it. The gas would expand my stomach and I would find myself eating more to fill it. I was starting to feel lethargic and toxic.

A couple weeks ago I finally did a five-day fast with a friend. I did a fruit and vegetable juice fast. I felt my body needed the healing. There are other fasts, but I much prefer the juice fast. I feel better. I feel my body gets some nourishment along with the cleansing.

My favorite book on juice fasting is Juice Fasting by Dr. Paavo Airola, published by Health Plus. I feel great, I dropped nine pounds, and I stopped eating chicken. I no longer feel bogged down in gunk. My thinking is clearer, my dreaming is more active, or at least my ability to recall my dreams has improved.

I have met people on this path who believe that food has only the power you give it. I knew one such chap in Southern California. He would declare with every bite that what he was eating was making him thin. I watched this guy consume obscene amounts of food and foods with a fat and calorie content that was off the chart. I wanted to kill him. Sure enough, he was losing weight.

What I discovered two years later was that he had been taking enough laxatives to open his own pharmacy. A lot of that is going on out there. I have found the New Age community as riddled with eating disorders as the general population. I always believed them when they said it was their faith or their spirit guides or whatever that was allowing them to stay thin. I wanted it to be true. I wanted some hidden power somewhere to give me a hand because I was having a terrible struggle. I didn't know I was having conversations about mystical slimness with anorexics and bulimics.

Or the reverse would happen. Some respected mystic would be one or two hundred pounds overweight and nobody would mention it. Everyone would act as if the person really had his or her act together. Obesity is not having your act together. I'm not saying these people don't have great information, they do.

Many fine therapists I have known are obese and do a hell of a job with their patients. The problem is they can take you only so far. These people have hit a wall somewhere in their process.

If you are trying to deal with physical, mental, emotional and spiritual recovery, until they deal with their issues they can't take you beyond it. Shakti Gawain's latest <u>Out of the Garden</u> is terrific at showing how the human must be dealt with — even for healers—if you plan on moving ahead with your life on more than one level.

Now I know some of you already deep into metaphysics have become vegetarians. I applaud you. One caution I want to raise is that if you haven't taken the time to get some solid information on the basic nutritional needs of the human body, do so now. Low blood sugar can be real quicksand when it comes to living in the light.

I remember when I first tried to be a pure, non-lacto vegetarian. I was depressed a large part of every day. I tried meditating my way out, praying my way out, journaling my way out — the list goes on and on. Finally, I had a candy bar and got immediate relief, followed by a deeper depression, of course. But I had had relief, and I was back on the sugar train.

When I'm eating foods that are okay with my system, my cravings practically disappear. I need to qualify that statement. As long as I am also experiencing and expressing my feelings, my cravings practically disappear.

If your eating or lack of it is completely out of control, the odds are you will need to take drastic measures. Try treatment, Overeaters Anonymous, something that helps you bring the problem under control. Initially these methods will be rigid. Be patient with yourself. There will be plenty of time later on to become more flexible.

If, on the other hand, you are like a great many of us struggling with basic lousy eating habits, you do have some choices. You can take the drastic approach, you can take the "change one food a month" approach, or you can find an eating plan that you think you can stick to that is relatively easy to follow.

To get started, I would suggest the Pritikin diet or *Fit for Life*. These programs are designed to allow you to go on with your life. You can follow either plan in most hotels and restaurants.

If these are too main stream for you, you can move into the world of whole live foods or macrobiotics. If you can't decide between the two, take in a lecture on each of them or, better yet, a debate if you can find one. When I am on track I personally prefer a combination of the two.

A good book on macrobiotics is You Are All Sanpaku by Sakurazawa Nyoyti. Any book or cookbook by Kushi on macrobiotics and Macrobiotic Kitchen by Cornellia Aihara are excellent. One of my favorites on whole, live foods is Survival into the 21st Century by Viktoras H. Kulvinskas, published by 21st Century Publications. Countless other books on both subjects, I'm sure, are also good. If you are at a place in your process where you can let your higher consciousness do the choosing, then just show up at the rack and let it pick.

Regardless of what method you choose please BE PATIENT WITH YOURSELF. If overhauling all your eating habits at once seems overwhelming, just change a couple of meals a week. It's not too important where you are on the illness/wellness graph. It only matters which direction are you headed.

If you have health problems, take the time to get some information from a doctor. My choice here would be a holistic M.D. Not enough practicing physicians understand good nutrition. I have seen too many conditions improve by simple changes in diet and exercise.

Use journaling, affirmations and meditation to help you with your new eating plan. Those of you in twelve-step recovery can use the steps and the fellowship. Those of you who are new to all of this can seek out people who are trying to live the way you want to live and use them as support.

There are plenty of groups. Just drop in on your local health food store or New Age bookstore and read the bulletin board. All of this is much easier to do if you can get someone who is willing to do it with you, or if you can get support from people who have already done it. I wish you well with this because it is one of the backbones of my growth.

Need an example? On the very day I'm writing this, my meals are the following:

Morning: Four or five fruits. This morning was an orange, apple, half a grapefruit and banana. I also take a garlic capsule, a multivitamin and a Ginko capsule.

Lunch: I will have a salad of lettuce, spinach, grated carrots, chopped celery, garbanzo beans, half a dozen olives and raisins, with a light dressing of some sort.

Dinner: Tonight will be chili made with tofu, tomatoes, garlic and kidney beans. It's terrific. My wife makes it. Other dinners include stir fry's with vegetables and often some type of seafood and brown rice. Occasionally we have bean and cheese burritos with rice and beans on the side — beans cooked in canola oil, not lard.

Dessert: Usually fruit or Gise. Sometimes we have sugar-free cookies or cake.

The same rules apply with exercise as eating. Start slow. Some of us have to launch immediately into complete physical exhaustion. Many of us want to run a marathon the first week. Be patient. If you haven't exercised in a long time, see a doctor. Sports medicine doctors can be as good as holistic M.D's. Just be careful you don't get one who is supportive of you breaking world records at thirty-five.

I've done Nautilus, free weights, Universal, running, swimming, Stairmaster, exercise cycles, bicycling. Today, my favorite exercise is hiking in the hills and mountains nearby. A few miles out in the wide open spaces is good for my body and good for my soul. Now that I have a Self, I don't mind being out in vast expanse. I used to prefer constriction. Space made me nervous. I believed the smaller the location, the easier for me to control it.

My wife and I also belong to a health club, and I do the machines maybe once a week. I'd like to work up to twice a week but it just hasn't fit in lately. Occasionally we ride our bikes, but walking or hiking is the main one. It has proved to be much easier on my body than running. Funny, since I've been hiking, I haven't had knee surgery.

At age forty — when I first started to exercise — I didn't want to just be healthy, I wanted to be an athlete. I ran 10Ks,

13Ks, half-marathons, marathons. I bicycled in fifty-miler aces and I was starting to eye triathlons, which were just starting to gain popularity.

It wasn't enough to be healthy. I had to be more. It wasn't macho enough to tell people I walk three to five miles a day. Walking was for old folks. I now have it on the word of experts — walking is the best exercise — followed by swimming. You can always walk. You may not always be able to find water. Swimming bores me.

You may have to run the races, ride the races and do the triathlons. I think it's great if you can stay in your body. Be aware of the movement, your muscles, your breathing, being alive. While walking you can do Vipassana and pull yourself into your body. If your exercise doesn't allow you to be present, then in some regard you are no different than the junkie with the needle stuck in his or her arm. You are accomplishing the same thing — separation from self.

If your eating has been out of control and piled life-threatening amounts of weight on you, walking is definitely the way to go. Again, be sure to get medical advice from a professional. If you are ashamed of your appearance, walk where there aren't many people.

If you live where it isn't safe to walk — you might want to ask yourself why you live there in the first place. If you believe you can't move, get a dog to protect you, or at least one that looks like it will protect you.

(A relationship with an animal is a great test of whether you can allow yourself to be a human being. If you can't allow the dog to be a dog — then odds are you can't allow yourself to be a human.)

Because of my history, what I put in my mind is as important as what I put in my body. Is it okay to read a little fantasy, a little fiction and escape once in a while? You bet. A getaway now and then is terrific. I can only stand so much reality, so much time present in my body and I need a break. It's all too new and as a rule, new wears me out.

Having had a violent past I once loved violence in movies and books. Once free from drugs and alcohol, however, I expected myself and others to behave in a civilized way. Only now I'm not sure what that means. Supposedly, we are civilized, and yet the only solution the majority of our elected officials seem to find acceptable to a problem is to Bomb the Bastards.

I need to regress for a minute. One of the reasons bombing is an acceptable solution is that it gives us someone to blame who is exterior to ourselves. When we look to someone or something external to ourselves for our answers, we also look for someone or something external to ourselves to blame.

For the most part, for example, our war on drugs is a joke. We have identified the bogey man — he is external to us — it's those damn Columbian's. Get more men, more planes, more boats, and more guns to stop the bogey man from bringing drugs to our adolescents.

With a little research you will find that our government supports Asian governments that are steeped in drug smuggling. We don't go after them. We don't go after Mexico where money can buy you hassle-free passage for your drugs (recent events give me hope that Mexico is improving). We jump on Noriega for drugs because he was one of our puppets who got out of control. Hear what I'm saying. Officials say the problem is external, yet they don't go after many obvious facets of it.

A few tuned in people have continually pointed out that any market lives or dies by the law of supply and demand. Eliminate the demand, and the supplier goes out of business. In my opinion, the solution to the drug problem is politically unpopular because it will require twenty years.

We need to raise a generation of teenagers with self-esteem and provide countless opportunities for other citizens to improve their self-esteem. If we were to do this the demand for drugs would be nearly over.

You may not agree with me, but I hope you can see what is going on. If our children are choosing a drugged-up state of being — something is wrong here — not in Columbia! If you dried up every last ounce of drugs, the unhappiness of our children would come out in more violence, more sex, more crime, more early marriages, more child-and-spouse abuse — the list goes on.

If don't care about me, then I can't care about you **unless** I do it to the total exclusion of myself. That creates a very angry person in both of us and that anger will eventually come out somewhere.

Children who like who they are, who have retained most of their power from when they were small, have no desire to whack themselves out on chemicals. Now, if you are a parent of a whacked-out kid, this may be uncomfortable to read. It may drive you to deny all of it. If you can speculate for a moment that you did the best you could considering your own history and the information you had available to you, and the job you did wasn't sufficient, then maybe you and your child can start finding some answers together.

One of the problems with television news is that the majority of information supports our dysfunctional belief system. One of the definitions I use for dysfunctional is, "Not good for humans and other living things." Our politicians point to the bad guys outside our borders and we can relax.

We sure as hell wouldn't want them pointing their finger at us. Down deep I knew I was part of the problem, but I also knew I didn't have any tools to help me do anything about it. This left me overwhelmed — a very familiar state of mind from my childhood.

I have explained how we seek the familiar. Once I feel overwhelmed, it usually affects other areas of my life. For that reason, I usually suggest to people that under no circumstances should they ingest more than thirty minutes of news in a day unless they take action. In other words no more than thirty minutes total of print, radio, television.

If you watch, hear or read thirty-one minutes, sit down and write somebody a letter about what has upset you. Write to the television network. They used to count every letter received as a thousand letters. Their reasoning was that for every one person who held a specific view and would take the time to sit down and write a letter, there were another nine hundred and ninety-nine who wouldn't. Do you suppose there have been times when the networks have counted on that lethargy?

I have been told that Senate committees count every letter as fifty thousand. Think about it.... If letter writing isn't your thing, find another way to take action. Find a candidate that believes what you believe and contribute money, answer phones, fold mailers, drive people to the polls, hand out flyers, clean the campaign headquarters.

Start small. Find out who is on your local school board and whether you believe they are competent. If you don't, do something about it. Write a letter to the editor of a local paper. If you do want them on the board, help them at the next election.

Start small but take action. Any positive action will help eliminate the frustration, the sense of being helpless and overwhelmed. We have the equipment to take action. When we don't, we suffer as much as society.

I have known a great many people living in the light who pray for solutions. I support that, but I also believe that action must be taken along with prayer. We folks have a healthy interdependence on each other. We are designed that way to need each other. Some of the people I know who prayed but took no actions eventually found the absence of solutions undermining their faith.

Nothing visible was happening to support their efforts. There were more homeless, not fewer. Give an afternoon to one of the shelters in your area. Help if there is a group restoring old housing for the homeless. Take a blanket, a coat, some boots and give them to a shelter or a homeless person directly.

If the funds allotted for the homeless in your area aren't reaching the homeless — take action. Find out why not. Write letters to the paper. Raise enough hell and whoever is skimming off some of the money will head for the hills.

Take the light you are standing in and shine it on others. I pray for the day there are so many volunteers for the needy that no one knows what to do with them all. Take action.

Being in touch with your feelings — experiencing and expressing your feelings — will help you take action. The more you can care at a human level about your brothers and sisters, the easier it is to do something.

A caution I would like to put forth is that you don't paralyze yourself by getting caught up in the ideal, the perfect solution. I could sit around daydreaming that someday soon I will be asked to come to Washington, D.C., and appear before a Senate subcommittee on children. I spend a couple hours outlining the problems and the solutions to those problems.

In my dream the committee would go into closed-door session, only to emerge a few hours later with a bill that covers every point I made. The senators put the bill before both houses, and it passes immediately. The tax dollars begin to follow our children — our hope for a future.

But while I am sitting around paralyzed in my dream of the ideal solution, NOTHING is happening. Yes, I am sending a positive message out into the universe, but the universe is full of positive messages. It needs some help down here. If I go to work on my local school board or local 'anything', changes are going to happen — if only in the minds of the people I talk to.

If you have young children and are painfully aware that funding for children is constantly being cut... talk to your parents. If they are like the majority of grandparents in this society, they strut around showing off pictures of their grandchildren while voting against every bond issue that has anything to do with children. Try to enlighten them.

That was a long excursion. Well, it was all about taking care of ourselves. Now, for more about the 'garbage in'.

For a long time — in the beginning of my recovery from drugs and alcohol — I had no confrontation or communication skills. So my solution to problems was to creatively visualize the death or dismemberment of the person I thought was responsible for my troubles. Television, movies or books that

167

gave me an opportunity to vicariously view others "getting theirs" relieved some of the steam building in my boiler.

I read Sasha a story last night about a little tug boat that was unable to let off steam and so burst its boiler. The story as written isn't terrific. The concept is, if you get mad or angry you burst your boiler. But Tina and I embellish on some of the stories for children and they work out just fine.

"Rock-a-bye-baby" was a favorite for a long time. Sasha had to have it sung to her every night. I added a verse about how the baby landed in the hay and everybody was happy because baby was okay.

We hiked Sabino Canyon yesterday.
Sasha was too tired to walk so we
pushed her in a stroller. Within a hundred
yards, she was asleep. We crossed
four bridges that were inches above a
rushing stream. As we walked, Tina
and I talked about how beautiful it
was for Sasha to be asleep out there with
all the wonderful energy of the trees,
cactus, mountains and streams
surrounding her. As we neared the end
of our hike, Sasha awoke and informed
us she had seen her Didi in the stream
and her Didi had talked to her.

Eventually, getting relief in non-confrontational, non-communicative ways became as debilitating as being frozen in an ideal.

I was taking no action and pressure was increasing, not decreasing. Like so many things in life, vicarious action had worked for a little while, but as time passed, it was no longer viable in my life.

Sometimes the old methods cease to work when I make new discoveries. Sometimes old methods cease to work and I have to go hunting for something to replace them.

People raised by nurturing parents know how to take care of themselves physically, mentally, emotionally and spiritually — the rest of us have a lot of work to do. We are attempting to undo the neglect of a lifetime. It can be done! The results are terrific! Feeling whole is the greatest high I ever experienced.

13

IS SOMEBODY IN THERE?

"If you want enlightenment
— lighten up."

THE ABOVE QUOTE IS FROM DOCTOR PEEBLES, a spirit channeled by two people I know of in the United States and probably more. He is quite a character — delightful to spend time with. He is in complete agreement with those in the Inner Child Movement who think it's time to have fun.

This chapter is going to be my attempt to contact my higher self, Little Turtle, White Eagle, Great Snake the Shaman or whoever shows up. I have not attempted this before on a project of this size. Sure, when I write I try to get out of the way and let my 'self' be a conduit for the creative energy around me, but my rational mind is still in there helping and hindering.

This time I am going to try to get out of the way. I told Tina yesterday I was worried that whoever I contact would not be able to type, and I don't want to do this longhand and then have to type it. I hate typing from my longhand.

My inner child refused to let me type his chapter in I Got Tired of Pretending. He was afraid I would edit what he was saying. I know the spirits aren't afraid of my editing what they are trying to communicate. They don't want me to get out so they can get in.

The spirit is an addition, not a replacement. They understand that a little bit of whoever is doing the channeling usually comes through. Tina assured me that whoever chooses to express through me will not hesitate to use all my talents.

I woke up this morning afraid to try this. My higher self, the still small voice, said, "You have many beautiful things inside of you. There is no need to be afraid." I like that. In the past, my written communication with my higher self has been short exchanges, a sentence back and forth between us, a small paragraph.

A book that I like very much on contacting/channeling your higher self is Innersource by Kathleen Van de Kieft, published by Ballantine.

The most complete book I have read on channeling is Opening To Channel by Roman and Packer.

I may ask questions of whoever shows up if that is required. I am a touch typist so I can type in a semi-trance. One thing I have noticed with handwritten communication — my guides' handwriting is as lousy as mine.

Here we go....

I have now completed a tour of the house, telling Tina, who was leaving anyway, that I don't want to be disturbed. I then told Sasha and her babysitter Monica just to leave a note if they go somewhere. Then I looked for Innersource. That entailed a twenty minute search of bookshelves. Now, perhaps, I have run out of distractions. Actually I am never out of distractions. Right now I can think of three people whom I should call immediately.

Okay, trance time. Let's go for it.... If whoever comes through doesn't identify him — or herself by name, I probably won't push it. I will trust that my intuitive process is fine enough to not allow in anyone who doesn't have my — or your or our — highest good as an agenda.

Okay, I hear you... I was thinking about the lousy condition of the planet and the voice came through telling me that the consciousness of people today is higher than it ever has been which is why an abundance of light is beginning to shine into dark corners and illuminate the secrets.

Although it (the world) appears worse, that is deceptive. There has always been and always will be shadows and darkness. Salvation comes when it is the light that rules the darkness. Not only do plants grow in the light, people grow in the light.

There is nothing to be afraid of in the darkness. There is much to learn in the darkness. People create the majority of their own personal darkness to hide in. It is hard to keep another in darkness. The human spirit is powerful and will only tolerate so much oppression before it tries to break free. People adopt strange values in order to enable themselves to stay in the darkness.

Your belief in the importance of self-esteem, a human self is a great truth. You see people who feel unworthy are more afraid of the light than they are the darkness. There are two types of darkness — the one created by others and the one we create. Your perception of children raised in the darkness becoming addicted to the darkness is accurate. They will always be drawn to the darkness. When there is no self in the light you are not in the light you are still in a darkness disguised as light.

A prison is a prison is a prison. To walk with us, talk with us, laugh with us is only a part of life as you know it. It is but a dimension. You have the same number of dimensions as the earth — water, air, earth, fire — body, mind, spirit, feelings. Ask yourself where humans would be without fire and you will know where humans are without feelings. But as with nature there: must be balance. You are not to be ruled by any one aspect. Stop holding your breath and hurrying so fast. You have the strength and the time to complete this — speaking of balance, listen to your body and go to the bathroom. I will be with you and we will go on.

I am going to the bathroom, and when I return I would like you to tell me who you are? What is your purpose in my life?

I am back with a slice of apple, cup of tea and faithful dog.

The dog Brujo needed to be with you. He as with all animals is much more finely tuned to the energy of the spirit world. One of your greatest assets is also a handicap. The rational mind if filled with faulty information is a giant boulder on your back. Hard to fly with a boulder on your back. Let the rational mind do its work in the human arena where it senses you well. Let it not be a master. If you can accomplish this you will find your flights into the world of the spirit free and easy. It will be as easy as walking through a door. It is struggles with the misinformed mind that exhaust you. You said earlier in your book that life is difficult, but it is not meant to be a struggle. That is true. To struggle is to wrap your bonds tighter. To struggle is to farther reduce your air supply. To struggle is to turn the earth underfoot into mud. To struggle is to put out the fire.

The fire of children is reduced to a smoldering ember when the giants around them are afraid of fire. Without fire, without feelings there is no light. Fire has been used to cleanse, to

174

sterilize, to burn openings through all types of materials. Honor your fire, nurse your fire. Breathe of the fire. In its heat is life, life like you have never known it. Yes the light of the fire casts shadows but in those shadows is the truth of the human being that is unacceptable to the society, thereby being unacceptable to the whole of yourself if you worry about the pack.

Your sexuality hides in the shadows of the fire. Let it dance in the fire. Your life is to be lived there. We are but to tell you the truth of the path. Where the path is — where to put your feet — and how to dance the dance. You are man and you are woman. You have been both before and you will be both again. Let them dance in the fire. Locking your energy into caves is death. There is no dance in the cave. There is no song in the cave. There is no music in the cave unless you call upon us to help you push aside the boulder by confirming for you what you already know to be true.

Stay clear of the pack. The pack lives in caves. It is essential that you walk, sing, dance with your brothers and sisters, but they will be on the path next to you and the one next to that and the one next to that. You can look over and see each other as each walks their path. Not all bunched up, blocking the light. Wherever you are on the path today is where you are. You can stay, you can go backward, you can come forward. To come forward is the most frightening until you learn by practice the thrill of adventure into the unknown. We await you in the unknown. We have for you information about the path, words to the songs, dance steps. We have the ability to provide energy to make you feel strong when you are weak. In your book you speak of care of the body, care of the temple. It is a temple, it is a work of water, air, earth and fire. Man cannot duplicate it. It is a miracle. Breathe, slow down. We have plenty of time.

I would rather be doing this with a tape recorder. Then someone could just type it up.

Learn this method. There is much more to write in the days, weeks, months and years to come. Breathe.... relax.... I am here.... We are not done.... There is love and life and flowers and birds and mountains and fish and trips to the moon and oh so much more. I am Orion. I have nothing to do with the film company, thought you would appreciate a touch of humor.... I have nothing to do with Orion so stop worrying. I am yours. As Orion I am only yours. Of course my silver threads entwine with others — but as Orion I am yours.

Do you know little Turtle or White Eagle or Great Snake the Shaman?

All are your family. It is this family that calls to you now. You have enough information about earth families. Balance. Come spend more time with your spirit family. We know that when you found your human self you became afraid that if you returned to your spirit family you would lose yourself. Not true we are here to love and guide and sing and dance with your human. Despite anything you may have heard we have all had our time on earth. You need not fear your human. You need not hide your human. Your human is beautiful. Your human is God's song being sung for all to see. Do not ask your human to do that which it cannot. Accept the human strength and weakness. You would not go sit in a building on fire because the human, the body would be destroyed. The human fire, the feelings would return to the universe as the energy they began from. The spirit would use that energy to propel itself through time and space. Tell the human it is okay that it cannot go sit in a fire. It was not designed to sit in a fire. You were given a mind to figure out what to do with man-made fire and a spirit to figure out what to do with the fire of the universe. You know how to put water on some fires. We are here to help you if you need it to figure out which fires need water and which fires need wood.

I do not understand?

Much like the backfires used in an attempt to control forest fires people build backfires to try and control those around them when their fire is too bright.

When one near you is blazing at your fire you need water.

What is water?

Water is the action required to keep the backfire from cornering you in a cave.

What is wood?

When one near you is trying to light the fire of their feelings give them wood. Wood is fuel, wood is support, wood is sharing your secrets to make theirs less frightening.

I feel sometimes like I have a candle and sometimes like I have a blow torch.

Sometimes a candle puts off enough light to blind everyone in the room. Sometimes a blowtorch can barely penetrate the darkness.

More please.

When those gathered in your presence are ready and willing for adventure a candle will light the way. When those in your presence are afraid of adventure a blowtorch will not be enough light. There is being afraid and willing and being afraid and unwilling. A candle for the willing and a blowtorch for the unwilling. You want to know why waste time with the blowtorch? Because every now and then the unwilling get a flash of the path and step forward. If you possess a blowtorch and you do — ignite it and let it roar. It is not the roar that scares the frightened and unwilling. It is the light.

Why are we so afraid of the light?

When a stage in a theater is dark you can see no one. So if an actor or actress has to rearrange their costume they can and no one will know. They can make themselves what they believe to be perfect in the dark. They can dress themselves according to someone else's script in the dark. If a stagehand accidently turns on the lights then they are caught in mid-adjustment. Caught trying to be perfect. Which — when using the yardstick of never making a mistake — is not what being a human is about. Others can see you in the light. If you are happy in the light and they are afraid of the light they will try and turn out your light. They will attempt to send hateful energy your way. They will tell others of your secrets that show in the light. They will roll the boulder in front of their cave.

You speak of actors and stage. Was it your business?

No it was yours. I use what will make under-standing the easiest. This realm is not about deep dark secrets, and mystery and seriousness and password.. It is about laughter. Laughter. Given space for their fire the laughter of children can heal others. Your own laughter can heal yourself. Seriousness is fear in disguise. Remove the mask from the seriousness in your life and you will find a frightened child hiding underneath. You will find a child who learned how not to laugh. The child has been old too long. It is time for the child to be a child. It is okay to have your childhood now if you missed it when you were a child. Don't get buried performing in someone else's play, using someone else's script, playing by someone else's rules. Move at your pace. There is plenty of time.

Now you sound like Little Turtle.

Little Turtle is quite wise. Little Turtle's patience is legendary. Little Turtle gave you information a little at a time. He did not call in all of us and try and instill in you the ability to see in one week all of the truth you will ever need in your life.

And that truth is...?

We are made in the likeness of God. There is one mind, one source of energy and power, one womb from which we all have our being. We are the song and the dance and the laughter and the love of all life.

Who is "we"?

You and me. You dance on the ground. We dance in the stars. Your spirit soars with us in the stars. Our spirit strolls at your side on the path on earth. There are experiences on the physical plane that are yours and yours alone. There are experiences on this plane that await you. There is a map to your path. Your guides are your unseen but often felt interpreters of the map. Who has been the most powerful example of the world human — the world spirit?

Despite the books, the channeler's, the mystics, the psychics, the ministers, the therapists, the workshops — I would have to say my daughter, Sasha.

Exactly, pure of spirit, pure of heart. She has appeared in your life after you had the courage to use all of the tools to roll aside the boulder and step from the cave. The other teachers have taught you to not write a script for her. She can live in both worlds.

She was born into both worlds as we all were. She will never have to leave this world to survive in your world. She will not have the struggle of finding her human and her spirit and uniting them. The song of her childhood will be with her when she is ninety. She can hear the song of her grandmother Didi even though her grandmother couldn't sing the song herself. Let the next book be her book. If the world is safe for children then it is safe for spirits. Sasha can dance with the spirits. Thank your wife for her ability to help keep those doors open in your house. Her hunger for the light her absence of fear of the dark. Let your women move you forward. Those external to you and the one in you. Come dance. When you encourage men to dance you do right. Seriousness is fear. Fear that there is no solution that there is no answer, that one is unable to go forward. To all of the problems that plague man right this moment there are answers but they cannot be found in the caves......................

I am being blocked because Bob is uncomfortable that I used the word man. There is no distinction here. We only make a distinction to make you comfortable. "The children will lead you," is a channeled truth. Provide them with a playground. From their playground will come the answers to those who are not blinded by the light of the children. Sing and dance with your children, your neighbors' children. Life is a gift, difficult, to be enjoyed. You cannot remove the shackles from the children until you first remove them from yourself. I am happy to have had this time with you. Come again when you want.

I thank you for your time. This has been quite an experience for me. I will now read what you have said. I still don't like the feeling of being out of control.

I have re-read this chapter and it is the first one in which I can find nothing I want to change. I will leave it alone. I particularly like the part about Sasha's being able to sing her grandmother's song. Sasha's book will be entitled <u>Walk Self</u>.

14

SIGNIFICANT OTHERS

Two halves make a quarter!

RELATIONSHIPS WITH OTHERS, PARTICULARLY significant others, fascinate me. It has been said of people with low self-esteem, "Let them get in a relationship, and it's like pouring manure on their character defects." Perhaps, but keep them out of relationships, and the sense of abandonment and loneliness is devastating. There is also the sexual acting out that can go on in an attempt to ease the pain of loneliness.

In the beginning, during the mating dance, people with low self-esteem are no different from anyone else in the ani-mal kingdom. They are on their best behavior and try to provide what they believe will keep the object of their affection hanging around. Of course there are exceptions — people who are so afraid of getting close that their worst behavior comes to the surface, people who have been so damaged as children that they run from closeness.

In I Got Tired of Pretending I entitled the chapter on relationships "Till My Past Do Us Part." The break-up of most relationships has very little to do with what is currently going on and just about everything to do with your or your partner's

181

history. It is those tentacles from the past that reach in and strangle the life out of today's relationship.

In an attempt to avoid doing the work required to find a self and learn how to communicate, people are getting joined in the spirit world by different names. They are having ceremonies performed by psychics in the realm of the psychic. They are getting joined a second time, in a special ceremony so they can be together in eternity. A lot of beautiful, interesting, exciting ceremonies are being performed.

Some of the participants, having done their family of origin work, participate in these ceremonies as part of the continuing adventure. Others hope to save their relationship. If the passion has died, love has cooled and the two of you communicate better with strangers – my experience has been it's going to take more than a ceremony to make the relationship sing again. But, given a choice,

I would rather see a couple have a mystical ceremony on top of a mountain to save their relationship than have a child to save the relationship.

To have a partner to share the adventure of recovery with, a partner to share the journey into the light with is a wonderful experience. It can also be a wonderful experience alone. I have had great times on this path both with and without a partner. Each circumstance has its own set of joys and its own set of problems.

When I wasn't acting out sexually, being alone usually afforded me more time to work on myself. By acting out sexually I mean using sex both with someone and in my mind as a means of avoiding my feelings.

When I was with a partner, there was usually more reaction than action. One or both of us would be in a strange state of being as a result of what the other had said or done or not said or not done. A lot of the time it was like being in a boxing match. Same principles. Drop your guard and you get clobbered. That perception was a tentacle from my past.

I have been married seven times. The women in my life, regardless of how it may have looked at the time, saved my life. When I needed another person to validate me, make me feel whole, they were there — most of the time.

I believe in relationships. I think they are terrific. I think it is important to understand that a relationship is a separate entity from the two people in it. It is not who they are. I don't believe that love of and by itself is enough. A relationship is like a car radio. Every time you drive through a tunnel there is interference and it is difficult, if not impossible, to pick up the station. There are many tunnels in today's world and too much interference to make it without both partners taking time to nurture the relationship to keep it growing.

I believe the purpose of a relationship is for each partner to help the other become the best, most powerful person he or she can be. I know that is childlike phrasing. There is something very childlike and wonderful about healthy relationships.

Tina was telling me a story this morning during breakfast. A young woman named Monica, a student at the University of Arizona, babysits for us often. Sasha adores her. When Tina and I did our workshop in Mexico for a week, we took Monica with us. Monica has a pleasant young man for a beau. The other day Monica came by with Jim. She wanted him to see the house and some of my wife's artwork.

Once the tour was over, it came up that Jim has great difficulty with the fact that Monica still has her childhood blanket with her. Tina went immediately to the closet and got out "Doggie." Doggie has been with Tina since she was a little girl. Tina explained that Doggie had slept with her until five years ago when she was thirty-five (She still sleeps with a variety of stuffed animals). Tina said there is a part of most, if not all, that needs the fulfillment of a childhood favorite. She told him that her husband (the one before me) had hated Doggie. In fact, one day she came home to find Doggie hung from a chandelier in the bedroom.

I, too, can remember being disturbed by anything my significant other showed affection to, or needed, particularly if I already felt inadequate. As a rule, we are filled with terrible information about our sexuality, about relationships, about the sexuality of our partner, even if he or she is the same sex.

The original information we got about how two people relate to each other came from mom and dad or their various partners. Some were single parents who sacrificed themselves completely for their children and had no partners.

The secret to healing relationships is the same as healing one's self. It is essential to heal the self to heal a relationship. Get information. Get books, go to workshops, work with a therapist. Often you will find you can say through a third person — things you can't say to your partner directly.

View the relationship as something separate and apart that needs its own time and care and feeding. Often Tina and I will ask ourselves what can we do at that very moment for the relationship. Sometimes it is as simple as taking a walk together to get away from child, phones, doorbell and any other distractions.

If you decide to try this, I can almost guarantee you that whatever you come up with, it will be inconvenient at the time. The trick is to do it anyway. Show the relationship it has value.

The business calls can be returned later, dogs can be fed later, the house can be straightened later and dinner can be started later.

Get a sense of how you feel about your body. That can have tremendous impact on a relationship. If I feel that parts of my body are dirty because my mommy told me so, I have created a massive problem for my partner. If my partner becomes involved with those parts, I think my partner is dirty and I don't want a dirty partner. I will begin to retreat from those activities. Sex becomes scarce. If I have good body and sexual-organ image, I can understand how someone would want to enjoy it.

If you are in a relationship but are not present in your body, it is like a premature funeral. Although in a survival state, having a partner as distant as we are can keep us alive. Once we make a decision to live, the same relationship is like an anchor.

Can you make a decision to find a self and step into the light and heal your current relationship? You bet you can. The catch is both you and your partner must be willing to do the work. If only one of you attends relationship workshops, only one of you will heal. The process is hard and rewarding.

When people begin to share the secrets they have kept for years about their needs and wants, it makes for fireworks. I do not believe we heal by hurting others. I don't think it is okay to say I had sex with your sister. I know some people believe you need to get all the secrets out of the closet and on the table in order to find out what you really have. I guess either way is fine. It depends on what works for you.

One of the problems I see in people who have moved into the light without bringing a self along is that they have no passion. It is as if they believe passion and spirituality are incompatible. Robert Bly, in <u>Iron John</u>, refers to what he calls

185

the soft male who has somehow trashed the wild man, trashed passion as a means of making up for the violence that men have inflicted on women, children and the world.

They believe if men can stay mellow, they will be doing an effective penance, thereby setting right the wrongs of generations of men. Not so. Leave your passion behind, and it sets you up for major passive-aggressive behavior. It incites others to anger while you keep your gloves spotless. You look wonderful while you set others spinning. Further, you can only suppress your passion so long before it comes seeping out the cracks in inappropriate behavior.

> *Sasha woke me up at the crack of dawn. Actually it was before the crack of dawn. She has a cough that woke her up. She wanted me to go into the living room and put the video of Peter Cottontail on for her. When I arrived back at bed, I found Tina on my side, having moved over intentionally to keep it warm for me. These are the kinds of things that she will do that makes my heart sing.*

A long-time acquaintance of mine who spent over half of his life in penitentiaries had his own rather crude philosophy on relationships: "If you ain't talkin' and you ain't fuckin', you might as well be hired help, 'cause you are selling your soul." Out of the mouths of babes.

Of course, there are exceptions. Some people get together and agree that sex just isn't in the cards. My experience with these couples has been that this arrangement is really okay with one of them but not the other. The other one's hormones arc still bubbling, and eventually they will boil over, scalding one or both of them.

As a rule, most of us go into relationships knowing what we want, need, and desire. The problem is that usually we keep the exact details secret even from ourselves. You might want to sit down and make a detailed list of what it is you want out of your relationship and your partner.

Be specific — how many times a week for sex, who does dishes, who cooks, who pays what, how many children, how much time alone, places you want to go with your partner, places you want to go without your partner, what kind of spiritual life you want and so forth.

If it will help, pretend you are writing a letter to God requesting exactly what you want. Sharing this list with your partner can really get things moving. I say this because usually we expect our partners to figure out what it is we want and need on their own — we expect them to simply know.

Don't be surprised — if you are honest with the list — that there are a great many things even you didn't know you wanted.

A good way to get on top of your sense of your sexuality is to write three letters. The first one is from your mother to you stating in writing whatever the message was she gave to you about your sexuality. The second one to you is from your rather — the same thing.

Now the messages they gave you may have been spoken or may have been by example. If they didn't talk about sex and didn't have sex, then perhaps the message was that sex doesn't exist.

If they didn't talk about sex but did it exist, this implied sex was an awful event that children shouldn't know was taking place, and perhaps the message was sex is dirty or shameful.

If the message was anything other than your body — all of your body — is a beautiful and wonderful gift from God — that your sex organs are as pure as your heart and meant to be treated with the same care — then you got faulty information. The third letter is to be from you to your parents, telling them the truth about your sexuality.

The letter writing alone will not make any problems go away. It will give you insight into what is going on. Like all phases of finding a self — of improving your self-esteem — it is necessary to go back and clean out all the feelings surrounding the information you were given and its impact on your life up until now.

It is terrible to have so little self that you must wait until your partner comes home to see how you are going to feel and what kind of evening are you going to have.

I know some of you who are steeped in New Age metaphysical work believe you can just magically make the events of your past and their impact on your life go away.

I have yet to see this be successful. I have watched people cut themselves off from their feelings and use all the wondrous tools provided in New Age work to stay cut off from their feelings. If that is what you want — go for it — but when light comes flooding in, there will be no shadow, and you haven't known loneliness like that.

I prefer to do the crying and dying necessary to experience the pain of the past, heal the past and move into the light. I have been blessed to have some terrific partners on this journey. At times we were feeding our addictions — but we were doing the best we could with the information at hand at the time. We were surviving... hoping that some day we could live.

15

THE TEARS

It's awfully hard to let in the new when the doorway is jammed with bodies from the past.

GRIEVING IS PROBABLY ONE OF THE MOST misunderstood activities that humans both participate in and avoid. Some cultures are better at grieving the loss of loved ones than other cultures.

When I say the doorway is jammed with bodies from the past — I don't just mean the bodies of people who are no longer part of our lives — but whom we have never really said goodbye to. I also mean the body representing our ability to trust ourselves and others that was taken/stolen from us as children.

There is a body representing the childhood many of us never had. We were old by the time we were four years old. There is a body representing our ability to love. There are bodies for our self, sexuality, self-esteem and the list goes on and on.

I appreciate the wailing of some cultures when they bid good-bye to a loved one. I used to hate it. It used to embarrass me. I didn't know how to act or what to do. I thought they were making a spectacle of themselves.

I now understand that some people wailing one loss were smart enough to include into that moment other losses, losses they had suffered in time gone by — but hadn't been able to grieve. Often in the cultures in which a good wail is allowed for the dead, no grieving is allowed for any other aspect of life.

It has been said that the end of anything is the tears. Until you cry the tears, you still carry around with you the person or event that has long since gone. Baggage is a great description.

I saw a play once entitled "Family Baggage?' It opened with a couple on stage, each carrying at least a dozen or more suitcases. One by one they tossed the suitcases to the stage floor, naming them — loss of self, trust, the burden of the family script and so forth. I used to show up at the apartment of my next future ex-wife for a first date and the ghosts of a dozen or more women would be standing behind me in the hall. Unbeknownst to me or my new love, I needed my new love to have a very large bed because they all were coming along for the ride.

I had never grieved the loss of any of these women — not even my wife who died after four months of marriage. I missed her. We were just getting started. If a relationship ended, and I suddenly found myself faced with feelings of sadness, I believed I still loved the woman and would move mountains to put it back together.

It was inconceivable to me that I could care about someone, care about the good times, miss her and still not have to be involved with her. In fact, if someone I was involved with started to share with me sadness over her last love, I would immediately remind her of what a jerk he was and how she was so much better off without him. I was threatened by her sadness. Obviously, based on my information, her sadness meant she was going to leave me and go back to the old beau.

What I know now is that my capacity to love the people currently in my life is in direct proportion to my capacity to grieve my losses. My capacity to love and live life is in direct proportion to my capacity to grieve.

This deep, black, dark hole, this self-pity (as the uninformed call it), this wallowing in the past, this weakness is one of the most powerful exercises I can participate in.

The power and energy I used throughout the years to repress my grief was monumental. Every bit of it reduced my capacity to be here, now and to participate in life.

Robert Bly and others in the men's movement talk about the necessity for men to learn to grieve. It is the biggest step we can take toward putting ourselves back together.

There are groups for grieving. There are workshops for grieving. There is a terrific book that you and one other person who is willing to grieve can do together. The book is The Grief Recovery Handbook by John James and Frank Cherry, published by Harper and Row.

I know many who just say this is the hand life dealt and want to move on. I know others who cling to the belief the loss is the best thing that could have happened to them. Still others believe the dead ones have gone to be with their maker and all things are in perfect order. All of this is fine for the intellectual mind, but it doesn't do a thing for the feeling human.

It is the feeling human that needs to be set free for the light to have any meaning. If you have begun to set your feeling human free, it is time to move into the light.

Lighten up. Sing your song, dance your dance, laugh your laugh, paint your paintings, write your poetry, write your music, sculpt your dreams, weave your rugs, sew your quilts, and bake your pottery. Or as Sasha says, "Walk self and fly to the moom."

SUGGESTED READING

Iron John by Robert Bly, Addison-Wesley.

Bradshaw: On the Family by John Bradshaw, Health Communications.

Healing the Shame That Binds You by John Bradshaw, Health Communications.

Homecoming by John Bradshaw, Bantam.

Don't Call it Love by Patrick Carnes, Bantam.

Out of the Shadows by Patrick Carnes, CompCare.

Creative Visualizations by Shakti Gawain, New World Library.

Reflections in the Light by Shakti Gawain, New World Library.

Return to the Garden by Shakti Gawain, New World Library.

Fire in the Belly by Sam Keen, Bantam.

Facing Codependence by Pia Mellody, Harper.

The Road Less Traveled by F. Scott Peck, Simon & Schuster.

Notes to Myself by Hugh Prather, Bantam.

Models of Love by Barry Vissell and Joyce Vissell, Ramira.

The Secrets of Life by Stuart Wilde, White Dove International.

The Trick to Money is Having Some by Stuart Wilde, White Dove International

Choicemaking by Sharon Wegscheider-Cruse, Health Communications.

Another Chance by Sharon Wegscheider-Cruse, Science & Behavior.

NOTES

NOTES

NOTES

NOTES

NOTES

Thank you kind reader and fellow traveler on this rocky road of recovery.

If you enjoyed this book and have found some benefit, please do leave me a review on Amazon.

It is these reviews that will enable others to find my books and hopefully move forward in their healing as well.

In Gratitude...

Bob Earll

For more Info:

BobEarllAuthor.com

TomAlibrandi.com

Made in the USA
Charleston, SC
08 December 2016